A Monk's Almanac

Celebrating
30 Years of Publishing
in India

A Monk's Almanac

Life Sutras for Troubled Times

NITYANAND CHARAN DAS

HarperCollins *Publishers* India

First published in India by HarperCollins *Publishers* 2023
4th Floor, Tower A, Building No. 10, DLF Cyber City,
DLF Phase II, Gurugram, Haryana – 122002
www.harpercollins.co.in

2 4 6 8 10 9 7 5 3 1

P-ISBN: 978-93-5699-432-4
E-ISBN: 978-93-5699-438-6

Typeset in 11.5/15.5 Warnock Pro at
Manipal Technologies Limited, Manipal

Printed and bound at
Thomson Press (India) Ltd

This book is produced from independently certified FSC® paper to ensure responsible forest management.

To Gaurang prabhu, my siksha guru, who has always held my hand and patiently guided me through all the ups and downs of my life

CONTENTS

INTRODUCTION

No one is spared in the world we live in. Who we are or what we do is immaterial. Despite our best intentions and efforts, we face disappointments and major setbacks in life. Sometimes we even feel miserable when we see others happy. But their reality is different. Everyone goes through pain. It is just not visible to us. Just because other people do not have the problem that we are going through does not mean they have no problems at all. They have another set of challenges to deal with, although they may not wish to show it.

TWENTY-FIVE PAISA CIRCUS

Once a circus came to a small village and everyone was excited. The amazing thing about the circus was that the tickets were cheap and economical. The cost was twenty-five paise only. A long queue of villagers could be seen outside the ticket counter. They were waiting from 5 a.m. onwards, even though the show was to begin at 9 a.m.

But there was a condition! Only one person could enter at a time to watch the show! The first person in the queue was feeling very fortunate as he would be the privileged one. While people pretended to glorify him, deep down, they were writhing in jealousy, wondering why they could not be the first one. At 9 a.m., the first person entered the tent. It was pitch dark. He waited for fifteen minutes, but there was no one around. Then he shouted, 'Hey, when will the show begin? Where is the clown?'

Suddenly, a huge wrestler appeared from one corner and said, 'The show will begin now and you are the clown.' He pounced upon the person and started beating him up. This went on for half an hour. Then, the wrestler threw the man near the exit, saying, 'Get lost.' The man was too shocked to protest. His hair was in a mess and his clothes were covered in dirt. He somehow stood up and was about to exit, when he remembered the entire village was waiting for their turn outside. They would make fun of him if they realized what had transpired.

So he dusted himself, combed his hair and came out smiling. Everyone was waiting in anticipation to hear about his experience.

'How was the show?'

He enthusiastically replied, 'Too good. Everyone must watch it. Do not miss it.'

And so, one by one, they went. Everyone got the same treatment but would come out smiling due to the fear of being made fun of.

In the evening, everyone met at the gossip corner and started discussing how good the show was.

Someone said, 'Did you see the magician?'

Another replied, 'Yes, yes, I did! It was very good.'

Then someone said, 'Did you see the size of the lion?'

Meanwhile, everyone thought to themselves, 'Only I have received the beating! Others have watched the show? How unfortunate I am.'

This is how our society works as well.

And this is the lesson we must take from this story. Everyone is wounded to some extent, although no one wants to show it because we are living in an age of exhibition. We try to impress others and, in turn, get impressed by others.

Lord Krishna says in the Bhagavad Gita. 'From Lord Brahma, the first created being within the universe, to an ant, everyone struggles in this world. Just that the nature of the struggle is different.'

The world is ever-changing. No situation is permanent. Even when we think our life is perfect with everything going our way, it is imperative to remember that the situation can change at any moment.

Does that mean we cannot do anything and like programmed robots, should just surrender to destiny? Not really!

The Ishopanishad says,

om purnam adah purnam idam
purnat purnam udacyate
purnasya purnam adaya
purnam evavashisyate

(God is perfect and complete, and because He is completely perfect, all emanations from Him, such as this phenomenal world, are perfectly equipped as complete wholes. Whatever is produced of the Complete Whole is also complete in itself. Because He is the Complete Whole, even though so many complete units emanate from Him, He remains the complete balance.)

The Lord is complete and so is His creation. There are no loopholes.

This means, for every problem, there exists a unique solution. If there are problems, there must be solutions as well.

Owing to my interactions over the last ten years, with people ranging across diverse age groups and backgrounds, I have zeroed down upon twelve problems that are common among all. Everyone keeps encountering these challenges daily.

I present in this book lessons to help the reader navigate through tough times in a more dignified way stemming from some in-depth knowledge of situations from our guidebooks, that is, the scriptures, guidance from my superiors at the monastery and experience gained through my own mistakes. Whenever the reader comes across a particular issue to deal with, they can just pick up this one book and find direction and solace.

The book discusses each problem in detail and the best possible response. The reader might find repetition in the solutions to various problems discussed. These are simple practices that needed to be emphasized and work for a variety of issues similar to a painkiller that could be a cure for pain in any part of the body. The nature of the problem, the cause and the effect with appropriate anecdotes, case studies, real-life examples, and, most importantly, the possible solutions/guidelines based on contemporary and ancient wisdom from the Vedic scriptures. Hope it adds some value to everyone's life.

Pain is inevitable. Suffering is optional.

What happens to us is destiny. How we respond to it is a choice.

Each chapter has, in the end, a small poem encapsulating the essence. These are penned by a very young and extremely talented Radhika Anand. She is just sixteen but mature beyond her age. Hope these poems will help capture the message of each chapter in our hearts.

If this book helps in making even one person's life better, we will consider our endeavour a success.

Happy reading!

CHAPTER 1

MIND CONTROL: MANAGING OUR BEST FRIEND

> For him who has conquered the mind, the mind is the best of friends; but for one who has failed to do so, his mind will remain the greatest enemy.
>
> —Bhagavad Gita 6.6

Mind control is today's buzzword because of the crucial role it plays in deciding our level of well-being. Everything ultimately boils down to the condition of our mind. If our mind is in good shape, it will be like a beautiful lotus in muddy water—happiness and satisfaction will be guaranteed. However, if our mind is in a mess, even if we are surrounded by thousand reasons to be happy, we will be miserable.

The Ramayana describes Laxman and Meghnad's battle: Before every fight, Meghnad would perform a sacrifice that would give him invisibility power on the battlefield, thus inflicting heavy losses on the enemy. It was only when Vibhishana revealed this secret to Laxman that he could catch hold of Meghnad before the sacrifice and kill him. Similarly, our mind can inflict heavy losses on us if we do not know its secrets and take control of it.

In the Bhagavad Gita, Lord Krishna describes an uncontrolled mind as the worst enemy. An enemy can destroy us if undetected; worst still is the case when we consider the enemy our best friend. In the present century, poor mental health has become the biggest challenge. It will be the biggest killer, as per predictions, not just by the medical experts but also by Vedic scriptures such as Shrimad Bhagavatam, the Mahabharata and various Puranas. Hence, it needs immediate attention.

To deal with an enemy, we must first know its whereabouts, nature, weaknesses and strengths. Without being aware of these parameters, it is immature and, to an extent, foolish to think we can win. No sane person can do that. Guesswork will not do.

So before we understand and reveal how to transform our mind into our best companion, let us first understand its nature and workings. Only then we can successfully and faithfully apply certain sacred principles as a solution.

POSITION OF THE MIND

We have three bodies: the gross body (everyone can see), the subtle body (comprising mind, intelligence and false ego) and the spiritual body (the soul, that is, us and our real identity). The mind is part of the subtle body because while it is there, it cannot be seen, and what cannot be seen cannot be dealt with easily.

In the Vedic literature (Katha Upanishad 1.3.3–4), it is said

atmanam rathinam viddhi
sariram ratham eva ca
buddhim tu sarathim viddhi
manah pragraham eva ca

indriyani hayan ahur
visayams tesu gocaran
atmendriya-mano-yuktam
bhoktety ahur manisinah

(This body is the chariot and the soul is its owner. The buddhi or intelligence is its driver. The mind is its reins. The senses are the horses pulling the chariot. The objects of taste, touch, sight, hearing and smell are its path. Thus, the soul uses the senses as a means to enjoy worldly pleasures.)

THE MIND–BODY CHARIOT

Imagine a chariot driven by five horses with a chariot driver and a passenger on board. The five horses are the senses, the reins are the mind, intelligence is the chariot driver and the soul is the passenger. The chariot driver must hold the reins tight and control the horses so they do not go astray. But if the driver is weak, the horses will run amok and take the chariot to the wrong destination. Consequently, the passenger will get lost. Similarly, intelligence is superior to the mind and must control it. However, when intelligence becomes weak, the mind takes command over it. The function of intelligence is to know the difference between right and wrong, and then to do the right thing. But an uncontrolled mind does not let intelligence exercise its power and, in turn, leads to the road of destruction.

Human life is not a T20 or one-day cricket match but a test match where even a below-average play in the first innings can be turned around and can win in the second innings. No matter how many times we have failed or made mistakes in the past, the present always gives us the opportunity to turn our life around.

NATURE OF THE MIND

To subdue the enemy, it is essential to understand its strengths in order to prepare and protect ourselves. An uncontrolled mind is our greatest enemy. In fact, according to the Bhagavad Gita and Shrimad Bhagavatam, it is the only enemy of humankind.

To understand better, we must delve deeply into the intricacies of an uncontrolled mind.

From the Bhagavad Gita's perspective

Arjuna says in the Bhagavad Gita [6.34],

canchalam hi manah rishna
pramathi balavad dridham
tasyaham nigraham manye
vayor iva su-dushkaram

(The mind is restless, turbulent, obstinate and very strong, O Krishna, and subduing it, I think, is more difficult than controlling the wind.)

Arjuna has used four words to describe the nature of the mind:

Chanchalam: It means flickering/restless like a child or a monkey. It is like a restless child who cannot sit in one place for more than a minute or two. Similarly, the mind too cannot focus on one thing for long and keeps jumping around like a monkey, never satisfied with what it has.

Pramathi: It means turbulent. Even if everything around us is quiet and peaceful, the mind can create havoc. We might sit in the most tranquil environment, but the uncontrolled mind can drive us crazy.

Balavad: It means extremely powerful. Imagine a drunkard entering a beautiful garden and causing damage. Now imagine an elephant entering the same garden. The elephant will cause much greater damage than the drunkard. But when a mad elephant enters the garden, it can destroy the garden to the point of no return. The mind is that mad elephant.

Dridham: It means obstinate. The mind wants to do just the opposite of what it is told to do. If you tell yourself not to think of something, you will discover that you think of exactly that.

Arjuna says it is easier for him to control the raging wind but not the mind. We know how difficult it is to control the raging wind. For instance, even the most advanced technology cannot save us when a hurricane strikes.

Arjuna had demonstrated that he could control the raging wind when he won Draupadi's hand in marriage. He hit the bullseye by completely focusing on the eye of the fish hanging to a moving ceiling while looking down into the water. This established that he had no dearth of power or focus, and yet a man of such immense calibre confessed that it was difficult for him to control the mind. Further, the Bhagavad Gita (6.35) says, 'asammshayam maha-baho mano durnigraham chalam' (even Lord Krishna accepts that it is indeed very difficult to subdue the mind).

Extremely sensitive to sound

Sound vibration influences the mind and gradually starts manifesting in one's physical body as well. It also refers to the literature we read since it is nothing but recorded sound.

Once, a healthy boy was kept inside a room and given nutritious food to eat in the morning, along with a tape recorder consistently playing 'by this evening I will fall sick, by this evening I will fall sick, by this evening I will fall sick'! And sure enough, by evening, the boy was half dead. The advertising world works on this principle. By consistently showing us the same thing again and again, eventually a desire to acquire arises in us.

Does paralysis by analysis

The mind is so powerful that we can create, enjoy, experience and destroy things with our thoughts alone.

Once a man was driving at full speed on a highway, and his car broke down. Coming to the conclusion that he could fix the car if he had a jack, he looked around and decided to approach a few houses for help. As he was walking, he thought, 'What if they don't help me? What if they refuse to give me the jack? How cruel of them! How can such people even exist in society? Why shouldn't they help someone in need and so helpless? Ridiculous!'

Eventually, what had started as a simple request for help, snowballed into hatred and judgement. Angrily, he knocked on the door and when a person came out, the man said, without exchanging any dialogue, 'Keep your damn jack with you, I don't want it!' The house owner was shocked. With mind power alone, the man ruined his chances of finding a jack.

Our idle mind makes mountains out of molehills. We assume the worst-case scenario and think the worst of others. We focus only on the negative aspects because of our uncontrolled and untrained mind, which makes life a living hell.

A split personality

The mind is a wonderful servant and a dangerous master.

It is like a knife. A knife in the hands of a surgeon has the potential to save lives. But the same knife in the hands of a criminal can destroy lives. Similarly, a trained mind makes for our greatest friend, but when uncontrolled, it is our worst enemy.

A storehouse of past impressions and future desires

Our mind has two sections—the conscious and the subconscious—forming 10 per cent and 90 per cent of the whole mind matter, respectively. While we are primarily aware of the conscious section, the subconscious mind, which has been a storehouse of all our past experiences for several lifetimes, is often ignored, and this is where the problem lies. All our activities, thoughts and experiences are stored in the subconscious mind and occasionally pop up, much to our cluelessness about their source.

The mind is a hard disc in which immense data is stored and can be accessed whenever we wish. Past life regressionists can activate this section of the mind and, thus, be able to reveal a person's past and the origin of the present circumstances. The subconscious mind is what needs the most healing.

Can turn a perception into a reality

Nick Sitzman, a strong young man, worked as a train-service crew. He had everything: a healthy body, ambition, a wife, two children and many friends. However, Nick had one fatal flaw: he was a worrier. He worried about everything and feared the worst. One midsummer day, the train crew was informed that they could call it a day an hour early in honour of the foreman's birthday. Accidentally, Nick was locked in a refrigerator boxcar with no on-site workers around. Panicking, he banged and shouted until his fists were bloody and his voice was hoarse, but no one heard him. 'If I can't get out, I'll freeze to death in here,' he thought. Wanting to let his wife and family know exactly what had happened to him, Nick etched words on the wooden floor with a knife. He wrote, 'It's so cold. My body is getting numb. If I could just go to sleep. These may be my last words.' The next morning when the crew slid open the heavy doors of the boxcar, they found Nick dead. The post-mortem report verified that every physical sign of his body indicated he had frozen to death. And yet the refrigeration unit of the car had been inoperative, the temperature inside indicating fifty-five degrees. Nick killed himself from worry. He had not frozen but kept thinking he was and eventually died. His perception became a reality.

WHAT DO WE DO NOW?

Humans always have a 'choice' between an 'action' and a 'response'. Just because the mind is making our life hell does not mean it is the end. Mind is dead matter. Why should we, the conscious living beings, be controlled by some subtle dead matter? As mentioned earlier, the soul (we) is superior to intelligence which is superior to the mind. We must realize and exercise our full potential.

Based on years of research and personal experience, we have laid down some very powerful and time-tested tools to cure the restlessness of the mind. These principles are to be respected and practised even when things go your way so that you have enough strength to deal with them when they do not.

Starve the bad dog

Two dogs sit in our hearts and represent the good and the bad. The Bhagavad Gita, Chapter 16, describes this as the divine and demoniac nature. A good dog symbolizes qualities such as modesty, humility, compassion, selflessness, sacrifice and service, while a bad dog epitomizes envy, greed, pride, illusion, exploitation and selfishness. Starving the bad dog means learning to reject temptations, emotions, thoughts or desires based on negative traits. The more we starve it, the weaker it becomes and it eventually dies. But a notable trait is that the moment we begin to starve the bad dog, it begins to howl louder. However, that should not discourage us because eventually, when we stop feeding it, it will perish. Likewise, we must muster the strength to say no to all temptations in life. Like in a gym, we push ourselves against resistance to build muscles.

By being around good association and satsang (hearing the divine name, fame, qualities, pastimes and divine message of the scriptures in association with the devotees of the Lord), we can derive wisdom to deal with our own internal negativity. 'Sat' means eternal truth. It also means good and pure. So when we associate with the right kind of people, our good dog, our divine side, is nourished, while the demonic side, the bad dog, is starved to death. Every time we resist temptation or negative thoughts, we become stronger, and we grow weaker every time we give in.

Set your sails properly

Stress is defined as a gap between expectation and reality, and rightly so. We cannot change the reality, but we can definitely lower our expectations.

It is similar to a sailboat that depends on two parameters: the sails' direction and the wind's direction. While one cannot change the direction of the wind, one can definitely change the direction of the sails. In life, too, we come across situations that we cannot change. So lowering our expectations remains the only way to lead a peaceful life. For example, the most unrealistic expectation in life is to think that everyone should be happy with us, everyone should behave the way we want, or every situation should be extremely favourable to us. This is not conceivable because of the sheer magnitude of differences in people: their upbringing, their set of experiences, their beliefs, their level of intelligence, their struggles, everything. Expecting them to behave just as we want is a sure-shot path to disappointment. By accepting the reality and reducing our expectations, we save ourselves from unnecessary anxiety.

Focus on what you can

There is a circle of influence and a circle of concern. The circle of concern encompasses things we have no control over: other people's behaviour, reaction or response to certain situations; what they are doing or what is happening ten thousand miles away. The circle of influence encompasses things upon which we exercise complete control: our response to things, our growth, our behaviour and our values.

An astonishing thing about these two circles is that they can contract and expand. The nature of the mind is such that whatever we choose to focus upon expands its horizons. Hence, focusing on things beyond our control, that is, in the circle of concern, is a recipe for disaster. On the other hand, by learning and subsequently disciplining our mind to focus on the circle of influence, we can lead a peaceful life. Gradually letting this circle expand assuredly grants us immense peace.

We, as monks, also sometimes face much hostility from people based on envy because not everyone can be happy with us, no matter who we are and what we do. In the past, it would disturb me for a prolonged period. However, one day I decided these people did not deserve my attention and energy. 'What am I doing?' I asked myself. 'I cannot change them. It is not in my control. I have to focus on what I am supposed to do and not on what they are doing to spoil my work.' As soon as I shifted my focus from them to my service to the Lord, I experienced tranquillity and exponential growth in whatever I was trying to do by God's grace. We should not allow others to sap our energy. If we use our energy to focus on things within our control, our circle of influence will get bigger and bigger to such an extent that the circle of concern will become literally non-existent.

Affirmations

A few years back, a major change occurred in my life, and things became topsy-turvy. For three days, I was in a deep state of shock and wondered what would happen now. Suddenly, by God's grace, a thought came to my mind. I realized the situation I was thinking about and worrying how I would manage was likely to happen in the future. It had not manifested yet. I realized that my thoughts were the only thing really causing me anxiety, so I decided to simply change them. The uncontrolled mind will always focus on negative prospects. But there is an equal probability that what we are worried about might not happen. Is it not? So why not focus on the positive probability?

I chanted to myself, 'It is a blessing, it is a blessing, it is a blessing'. I chanted two to three sets a day and five to six times in a set. Amazingly enough, to this day I cannot remember when that problem or anxiety disappeared. This holds a simple logic: my anxiety stemmed from my thoughts alone and not from the situation. When I took care of it with some positive affirmation, it, in turn, took care of my stress. Affirmation really helps. Each one of us can have our own affirmations. The first thing after waking up and the last thing before sleeping should be our affirmations. The affirmations can be tailored to suit our needs. Repeating positive sentences in our minds helps us focus on the positive side of life.

For example, instead of analysing and paralysing ourselves when someone's behaviour bothers us, we can think, 'Everyone is nice, everyone is loving, everyone is kind' or we can focus on one good quality that the other person has. We will be surprised at what this simple technique can do. Immediately, we will experience a shift in our consciousness. Mind you, while they have not changed, they no longer now have the power to make us anxious or angry. We have taken our remote control back from them.

Unless a situation manifests, why unnecessarily worry about it?

Put the glass down

A professor began his class by holding a half-filled glass of water.

He asked his students, 'How much do you think this glass weighs? 50 grams! ... 100 grams! ... 125 grams?'

The students said they could not say unless they weighed the glass.

The professor asked, 'What would happen if I held it up like this for a few minutes?'

'Nothing,' the students replied.

'Ok, what would happen if I held it up like this for an hour?' he continued. 'Your arm would begin to ache,' said one of the students.

'You're right. Now what would happen if I held it for a day?'

'Your arm could go numb. You might have severe muscle stress and paralysis and even end up in the hospital!' ventured another student making everybody laugh.

'Very good. But during all this, did the weight of the glass change?' the professor asked.

'No,' came the reply.

'Then what caused the arm to ache and the muscle to stress?'

The students looked puzzled.

'What should I do now to come out of the pain?' asked the professor again.

'Put the glass down!' replied one student.

'Exactly!' said the professor.

When somebody abuses or insults us, we will experience the pain only if our mind holds onto those words. The longer we hold on to them, the longer we will experience the pain. Hold for a few minutes in your head, and they seem okay. Think of them for a long time, and they begin to ache. Hold them even longer, and they begin to paralyse you.

By learning to let go of negative thoughts, abusive words and insults, we will be saved from unnecessary problems in life. It is for our benefit, peace and happiness. By doing this, all we will lose is unnecessary anxiety and baseless arguments. It helps to remember that how people treat us is a statement about them, not us. What people think about us and who we actually are could be two different things. Thus, when somebody respects us and is nice to us, it shows that they are nice, whereas if somebody insults us, the problem, somewhere deep down, lies within themselves. Neither has got anything to do with us. This principle helps us remain happy, satisfied and stable across all kinds of situations.

Focus on your blessings

Life comprises good and bad situations. What we choose to focus on decides whether we are happy or miserable.

Time and again, the philosophy of writing down blessings has proved to be immensely beneficial. Anything written down, anything in front of our eyes, has a greater impact. Put the writing in a place where it is visible and read it at least thrice a day: once in the morning after getting up, once during the day and before going to sleep.

By this, we are reinforcing the positive side of life and focussing on the good. Gradually, the mind begins to believe this and starts manifesting even more of it. The opposite also holds true.

Focus on your needs

There is a difference between what we need and what we want. According to the Bhagavad Gita, humans are spiritual beings and so our needs are also eventually spiritual. Our list of wants may never end, but by learning to focus on what we actually need rather than what we want, we can lead a peaceful life and the mind can also experience greater satisfaction. So, whenever a desire arises in our heart or mind, we should introspect, 'Do I really need it?'

When buying things, we should ask ourselves, 'Do I really need it?' If we get affected by our neighbour's wealth, we should think they might have it, but do I need it? Looking around, we will see that we have enough to lead a happy and peaceful life. Even if somebody is earning one crore rupees every day, he will still only eat three to four chapatis in a meal and need a small bed to rest.

Give positive instructions

We should tell the mind what to do rather than what not to do. A more positive approach is needed to deal with an uncontrolled mind.

Once there was an eight-year-old boy. As a kid, he was always found climbing trees and poles and literally hanging upside down from the rafters of his lake house. So, once it came as no surprise for his dad to find him at the top of a thirty-feet-long tree swinging back and forth. His little eight-year-old brain did not realize that the tree branch could break or he could fall and get hurt. He just thought it was fun to climb up so high. His older cousin had also climbed the same tree. She was hanging on the first big limb, about ten feet below him. The girl's mother also noticed them at the exact time as the boy's dad did. Right at that time, a huge gust of wind blew. The boy could hear the leaves rustle and the tree sway. The boy heard his father yelling over the wind, 'Bart, hold on tightly.' So he did. The next thing he heard was his cousin screaming at the top of her lungs. She had fallen from the tree. The boy climbed down the tree to safety. The boy's father later told him why his cousin fell while he did not. Apparently, when the girl's mother felt the gust of wind, she shouted, 'Don't fall!' And the girl fell.

The father then explained that the mind finds it difficult to process a negative image. For the girl to process the command of not falling, her nine-year-old brain had first to imagine falling and then try to tell the brain not to do what it had just imagined. On the other hand, the boy's eight-year-old brain instantly had an internal image of him hanging on tightly. We cannot visualize not doing something.

Raise yourself to a spiritual platform

The mind tricks us, but there are principles to help us trick the mind. One eternal principle that can help us deal permanently with the disease of the mind is *rising above* by increasing our spiritual depth. How can we achieve that?

Sharpen your intellect. Intelligence is superior to the mind and, hence, it can control the mind completely. But if intelligence gets weakened and the mind stronger, the mind will take the upper hand. We can sharpen our intelligence by regularly hearing or studying the scriptures. Just like a sharpened sword's heightened impact, a sharpened intellect aids us in making the right decisions.

Not long after I joined the temple as a full-time monk, one of my first services was to receive guests, interact with them and offer them prasad. However, as we come in contact with people who carry different types of energy, many times negative, we tend to get affected and thus end up experiencing turbulence in our mind and feeling distracted, depressed and low on energy. It was one of those days when my mind was going insane and driving me crazy. However much I tried to keep calm, I failed. Then by Lord Krishna's grace, good sense prevailed, and I picked up a book based on the Bhagavad Gita. And after reading two pages, I felt so calm that I do not even remember to date what had bothered me in the first place. Scriptures are recorded sound. When we allow our mind to come in touch with divine sound, it gets cleansed of all negativity.

Awaken the soul. In Sanskrit and Hindi, the mind is known as 'mann'. It is in the form of a mantra. When we have a cold or a cough, we get appropriate medicines. Similarly, the scriptures are the guiding books for humankind and prescribe the best medicine to deal with the mind or mann.

Mantra means 'manas trayate iti mantra'. In other words, that which liberates the mind is called a mantra. When we chant the holy names of God, specifically the Hare Krishna mahamantra ('Hare Krishna Hare Krishna, Krishna Krishna Hare Hare; Hare Rama Hare Rama, Rama Rama Hare Hare'), as recommended in the Kali-Santarana Upanishad, and meditate on the sound of the mantra, it enters through our ears, goes to the heart and mind and cleanses them completely. Just like a detergent powder forms a layer around the dirt and pulls it out. Chanting the mantra is the most powerful way to deal with the mind and completely cleanses all impressions from the subconscious mind, the root cause of all anxiety.

Being a monk is not easy. There are challenges just like anyone else has. The only difference is the nature of the challenges. Our major and only challenge is our mind. In the Bhagavad Gita, Lord Krishna mentions mind control as one of the most important aspects of yoga or the process of linking with the supreme. It was a few years after I became a monk that I experienced a turmoil. As we are conditioned souls carrying various vices in our hearts, after becoming a monk, we try to recondition ourselves, which is a challenge. I had heard devotees quoting many scriptures about the power of chanting God's names (such as the Hare Krishna mahamantra) and I decided to try it out sincerely and put in a conscious effort. Not that I was not chanting every day my prescribed number of rounds, but I was distracted. So I decided to chant with concentration. Our mind is such that if we give it a long-term task, it projects it as a mental burden. So I decided to make its job easier. In essence, I decided to trick the mind. I told myself, 'For the next three days, and not any longer, I will focus on the sound of every mantra (there are 108 repetitions in one round. I chanted [still do] sixteen rounds).'

As I followed this regime and focused on the divine sound of God's names, miraculously, on the second day, I became free from all worries and felt absolutely fine. While the same old problems were still there and the situation around me had not changed, I was not affected by them at all. The chanting can really uplift the state of our mind in no time. It puts us in a different zone.

Imagine standing outside on a hot summer day. Again imagine being in an air-conditioned room. Do we still feel the discomfort? Not at all! Has the outside temperature changed? No! But we are not affected because we entered a different zone altogether. We cannot change the environment around us. But we can certainly rise above it. And chanting the Hare Krishna mahamantra can do wonders to achieve this goal.

Lord Krishna says in the Bhagavad Gita (2.70),

aapurya-manam achala-prathistham
samudram apah pravishanti yadvat
tadvat-kama yam pravishanti sarve
sa shantim-apnoti na kama-kaami

(A person who is not disturbed by the incessant flow of desires—that enter like rivers into the ocean, which is ever being filled but is always still—can alone achieve peace, and not the man who strives to satisfy such desires.)

A SPIRITUALLY EVOLVED PERSON BECOMES LIKE AN OCEAN

During monsoon, gallons of water falls into the ocean and during summer, gallons of water evaporates. However, the ocean remains unaffected in both situations. Why? Because of its enormous depth. On the contrary, a hole easily gets affected. During the rainy season, it gets immediately filled, and during the summer, it gets dry. Why? Because it lacks depth.

The Bhagavad Gita explains that our true identity is to be spiritual, which implies that the spiritual environment is our natural environment. The more we try and increase our spiritual depth, the more we can remain undisturbed in all situations. The mind goes through hankering and lamentation because it seeks fulfilment. However, we must know that no amount of material arrangement can satisfy our hankering as it is an incompatible situation, because a spiritual being is trying to find happiness in matter. If we wish to experience everlasting happiness, then we need to start seeking it in things that are of similar nature, that is, spiritual.

The famous nutritionist Rujuta Diwekar makes an interesting point. She says that no matter which part of the world we are in, we must eat the food of our native land because that is natural to us, and our bodies have been designed to eat and feel nourished with that food. That will keep us healthy.*

Just like there is food for the body, there is food for the soul. We are the soul. We are spiritual, and we should keep eating such food regularly. Lord Krishna tells in the Bhagavad Gita that the mind can be subdued through practice and detachment. Practice involves applying the principles discussed in this chapter, and detachment is not getting affected or discouraged by the apparent failures as we try to accomplish this humongous task. We will fail sometimes, but if we continue the practice with determination, eventually we will succeed, or at least reduce the damage to a considerable extent.

---

* *Indian Superfoods: Change the Way You Eat* (Juggernaut, 2016).

IN A NUTSHELL

In a dark room, a mind is astray, detecting direction in dismay.

An uncontrolled mind, thoughts are at feud, ensued turbulence, intelligence subdued.

Sowing the seeds of self-sabotage, trapped in the loop of flogging a dead horse.

Haven't we discerned the dupe of overthinking arouses remorse?

However, every action and reaction is bounded by a defined choice.

The decision of taming or tormenting the mind, being damaged or divined.

The depletion of obstinateness in exchange for peace in life.

Wishing goodbye to the strife by taking control of the empowered mind.

It's the double-edged sword depicting rivalry or amity, is the mind a friend or an enemy?

As a nemesis, it's a hassle, what's the point of fighting a losing battle?

As an ally, it's an ace up your sleeve, why wouldn't one want to achieve tranquillity?

Chant the Lord's name, surrender to God, He will purify the mind, as a reward.

A controlled mind, liberated soul, by the grace of God, protested happiness transpired to my door.

CHAPTER 2

RELATIONSHIPS: THE SACRED THREAD

Everything that we do in life is to become happy. When someone says their goal is to be an actor, a sports star or to be wealthy, it is not these states they covet, but the happiness derived from them. If these activities do not make us happy, we stop doing them. However, it has been proved time and again that money, acquisitions or achievements do not equate to happiness. Happiness can be found in the poorest corners or people and does not necessarily reside only in wealthy mansions or success stories.

However, there is one thing and upon having that, life can be relatively happier and more satisfying; it is 'deep, loving relationships'. Having the whole world means nothing if we do not have someone to share that opulence with! Happiness is only truly experienced when we have someone in life with whom we can share it.

The Vedic scriptures explain, 'eko vai sah'. The Lord was one, and then He expanded Himself into many parts and parcels to experience sweet loving mellows or relationships. It is proof that this is what makes Him feel complete. So what to speak of us! In the Bhagavad Gita, Arjuna gives the same reason for refusing to fight the war. He tells Krishna that even if they win the war by destroying the Kauravas and regain the kingdom, what use will the kingdom be when everyone—his family, friends and relatives—are gone because he was fighting against them. 'There would be no happiness', he said.

Relationships are the sacred thread that makes life and everything else beautiful. It is like the thread in a pearl necklace. Even though the thread is not seen, it is the most important part of the necklace. If it is not in place or is broken, the pearls will fall apart and the beauty of the ornament will be lost. Similarly, life's beauty and charm are lost when we lack meaningful relationships.

However, we live in the Kaliyuga, an age characterized by quarrel, disagreement and hypocrisy. The odds are stacked against us. As a fire can erupt in a forest from a tiny spark between two dry woods, no human effort is required to start a quarrel in today's day and age. It happens naturally. People fight on non-issues. A structural engineer works hard to make sure the structure he is erecting stays intact as he has to work against the law of gravity. Similarly, in an age where everything is going downhill in terms of values, tolerance levels, spirit of compassion and sacrifice, we need to work overtime to sustain everything, especially our relationships.

With the passage of time, a different scenario is manifesting—'Love at first sight, divorce at first fight'. In our tendency to be influenced by external matters, we tend not to notice or overlook each other's faults in the initial stages! On spending time with each other, everything comes to the surface! We are taken by surprise by the reality as we had concocted a totally different picture in our mind. And our natural response is anger, resentment, frustration and denial. However, as humans, we always have the free will to choose a better response and rectify the situation.

Before we discuss how we can respond in a more dignified way, we will first examine certain factors detrimental to long-lasting relationships. Before being prescribed the cure, we need to understand the causes of the disease.

WHY DO RELATIONSHIPS FAIL?

Lack of communication

In a world where we desperately try to be understood, we forget to be understanding. Communication is the heart of relationships. And a lack of it is the killer.

A couple came to a marriage counsellor in tears. They had been arguing for weeks. Each took their turn to explain their issues. Several sessions passed discussing the harsh words and mental pain they had both suffered. The counsellor was looking for an underlying cause for this breakdown.

Finally, the husband was beside himself with anger and frustration and blurted out, 'She has absolutely no respect for me. My ego cannot bear it anymore'.

The counsellor continued, asking, 'Can you remember a time or event when you first felt this feeling towards her?'

He answered, 'Yes, every day during breakfast, she gives me the end part from a loaf of bread. Why doesn't she give me the good bread? In my family, we would feed the dry, crusty end pieces to our dog or threw them in the trash. This is an insult!' The wife, visibly shocked by his words, burst into tears and exclaimed, 'Where I come from in Italy, the end parts of the bread are considered to be the best part. When I grew up, my family would fight for them. To respect my husband, I sacrificed my enjoyment every morning to give him the end portion. I'm sorry, I didn't understand.' The husband was from the USA, while the wife was from Italy. Realizing his mistake, the husband said, 'I'm sorry I didn't understand you.' This is how a lack of proper communication between two parties can prove to be disastrous.

False ego (I, me and mine)

In the above story, beyond miscommunication resides a much bigger, underlying problem: the tendency to place oneself at the centre. The tendency to feel what I think and feel is 'the only right' springs from a deep-rooted false ego.

Imagine we are sitting on a river bank. We pick a pebble and throw it into the water. It hits a particular point on the water's surface, and beautiful ripples get created. Keep hitting the same centre and we see similar ripples. However, if we hit different centres with different pebbles, the emerging circular ripples will collide. Similarly, we can expect collision if every party wants to be the centre and be seen as important. Research has also shown that people who only think about themselves are the most miserable and prone to mental illnesses, with depression being the most common one.

Misunderstandings

Often, while there is proper communication between two people, a point trying to be conveyed by one party might have been missed or misunderstood by the other due to lack of attention and maturity, a different personality or not having received the communication at all.

This usually happens when we send a text message to someone and they do not reply. We wait to a point and then arrive at a conclusion within the confines of our minds and decide to hold the person in a bad light.

Even a monastery is not bereft from such kind of miscommunication. I once messaged a devotee about a requirement as he was in charge of the temple residents. It was a desperate situation. When I received no reply for three days, I decided in my heart that he was living peacefully and did not even have the courtesy to reply after so long! This was unacceptable to me. I decided to keep my distance from him and expressed my problem to a senior devotee. The senior devotee spoke to this devotee. The devotee was surprised and phoned me immediately. He had not even read the message. He generally checked WhatsApp messages and I had sent him an SMS. I forgot that many times, even I do not read an SMS. And it is never deliberate.

When we judge others, we do so by their actions; when it comes to us, we want to be judged by our intentions. It should be the other way around.

Another incident that comes to mind is of a lady who attended a few sessions of my class many years ago but stopped abruptly. It did not make me happy and I thought she was not interested in my classes. One day she called and wanted to visit the temple for darshan. She came with a few presents for me and lovingly handed them to me. As we sat down to chat, what she divulged taught me a powerful lesson: never judge anyone! I had totally misunderstood her. She informed me how much she liked my classes and wanted to continue but could not as she had a grown-up special child to look after. She explained her struggles as a mother and the problems the family faced when they first came to the city. Listening to her, I could barely manage to restrain my tears.

There is always, always another side to the story. It may be completely contradictory to ours, but that another person deserves a fair chance to explain. There are several reasons why you did not receive a reply to your text message. Maybe they were not in good health or were busy and waiting for an opportune time to reply or they had typed the reply but missed sending the message (yes it can happen and it happens more often than you'd think). And the person thinks they have replied to your message. When we arrive at a conclusion without verifying the facts, it wrecks relationships.

Humans are not perfect. There are challenges. We all make mistakes. To err is human. But we are also blessed. Blessed with the ability to rectify the errors we have made. And we must exercise this potential to the fullest.

The way out

There are certain sacred principles that not only facilitate establishing a new relationship but also sustain an already established one and repair the damaged ones. As difficult or impractical as it might sound, remember that it is important for our own happiness. And it is no secret: we all know it.

No one is happy in a strained relationship. Each party keeps accumulating a lot of negativity, clogging their hearts and sapping their mental energy, which could otherwise have the potential to be used for some constructive work. Human life is meant for something higher and when we are together, we become most happy and when we are happy, we can pursue higher goals much more enthusiastically. Before we delve into the principles, we must make an important note: 'Relationships are not a one-way street. They are a two-way street.'

These principles need to be practiced by all parties involved and not just by one. If the relationship is our priority, we must be willing to make an effort and surely, we will be more than rewarded.

To love means to serve

If we love someone, we must serve that person and that service should be pleasing to the object of our service. If the service is not pleasing, it is not a service. And this service must be mutual. Any relationship that has service as its main foundation will be everlasting. When we serve someone, even if they are residing ten thousand miles away or even if we have never met them, we shall, in a short time span, develop a strong bond and when we actually meet in person, it would be as if we have known each other forever.

The nature of the soul is to serve. When both parties think about each other's happiness rather than their own, they find inner fulfilment and are on their way to a deeply loving and everlasting relationship.

Upon his death , a man was given a tour of both heaven and hell to select his final destination. First, he was taken to hell. He saw people sitting at a long banquet table filled with all kinds of delicious food. However, he noticed that everyone seated at the table was unhappy and looked frustrated. They each had a fork strapped to the left arm and a knife strapped to the right arm. Each had a four-foot handle that made it impossible for them to eat. Though every kind of delicious dish and delectable sweetmeats conceivable were in front of them, they were unable to taste any of it. After this scene in hell, the man was escorted for a tour of heaven. There he noticed that the people were also seated at a long banquet table filled with all kinds of delicious foods. But there was a difference. He saw that the people here were cheerful and enjoying themselves. They too had forks and knives similarly strapped to their hands. But they were busy eating because they were feeding each other. Each person in heaven was feeding the one sitting across the table and was being fed in return. The people in hell were unable to eat because they were trying to feed only themselves.

Depending on whether we are trying to serve or want to be served, we can create a heaven or hell for ourselves and for those around us. The choice is ours and ours alone!

Sacrifice

Nothing great has ever been achieved without sacrifice. Relationships are no exception. The ultimate sacrifice we can make is that of our false ego. False ego has destroyed many relationships. Relationships are fragile and have to be handled with care. A 'my way or the highway' approach is bound to come to a bad end. Everyone thinks that they are right and that right is the core of the vicious, never-ending cycle of competition.

If we truly value our relationship, we must be willing to take a humble position. This, however, gets most difficult when we are absolutely convinced that we are right.

Saying 'sorry' does not necessarily mean we are wrong. It simply means that 'we value the relationship more than being right'. We must choose our battles carefully. Not every battle needs to be won. In a battle of ego, the loser is always the winner. What do we lose by saying sorry even if it is not our mistake? Nothing except unnecessary argument and frustration. As soon as one party owns the mistake, the matter immediately ends there. Much energy is saved. One who bows down is the one who is great!

Once a demigod descended into Vrindavan. Everyone gathered to welcome him. Krishna's father, Nanda Maharaj, was also there and he bowed down to the esteemed guest. Everyone started loudly shouting, 'All glory to King Nanda! All glory to King Nanda!'. The demigod asked in surprise, 'I am the one who has descended from the celestial realm. I should be the one who receives all the glory. Why Nanda?' To that everyone said King Nanda was greater. 'Why?' asked the demigod. Everyone replied, 'Because he is the one who bowed down'. So whoever takes a humble position is the one who is actually considered great.

Once, I was travelling to Vrindavan with a family from Delhi. A thirty-five-year-young man was driving. I was sitting in the front and his wife and sister-in-law at the back. We were in Nandagaon (Krishna's village) where the roads were extremely bad. To add to it, it had rained heavily. As we were exiting Nandagaon, a truck approached from the opposite direction. Due to the truck driver's mistake, we had to stop. As the truck drew closer, we could see the driver was angry and was about to shout and blame us. As the truck came closer to the car, the young man immediately joined his hands in a gesture of apology and said to the truck driver, 'Sorry, it was my mistake'. The truck driver's demeanour changed as soon as the young man said this. He instantly calmed down and drove away, merely saying, 'Ok! Be careful always.'

All of us were shocked. His wife, perplexed, asked him, 'It was not your mistake, then why did you say sorry?' To which the young man simply replied, 'If we say sorry, the matter ends then and there itself. What did we have to lose?'.

This offers a powerful lesson: avoid unnecessary arguments by letting go of your ego.

Sometimes, to satisfy our big, fat false ego, we do not realize the staggering amount of anxiety we invite into our life. In a city lived a couple who constantly quarreled. In their neighbourhood lived another married couple quietly and happily. They would often feel jealous of them and their peaceful home. Once the wife told her husband, 'Go to the neighbour's house and find the reason for their well-being.' The husband went to their neighbour's house and hid outside. He saw a woman wiping the floor in a room. Suddenly she ran to the kitchen. Listening to the noise, her husband too rushed into the room. In his hurry, he did not notice the bucket and accidentally kicked it. The water spilled onto the floor. A few moments later, the woman came back and noticing a wet floor said to her husband, 'I am sorry, it is my fault. In my hurry, I forgot to remove the bucket from the way.' To this her husband replied, 'No, it is my mistake. I should have noticed it. I am sorry for not noticing it and spilling all the water.' After this exchange, they cleaned that water together and continued their day. The husband came back to his house and narrated this to his wife. The wife asked him, 'Did you understand the reason for their well-being?' He replied that he did. 'You see, in our home, both of us always seem to believe that our own actions are right and blame the other for any mistake. In contrast, in their house, both take the blame and work together to correct whenever something wrong happens.'

It is our decision: Do we want to win the war of ego and lose the person, or lose the war and win the person?

Spend time

Out of sight is out of mind.

Spending quality time together strengthens and deepens a relationship. To love and be loved is the need of every soul. Our time is the greatest gift we can give to someone to show how much we value and care for them.

There have been countless examples where the relationship fell apart despite having all the luxuries because the couple did not give each other time. We are supposed to love people, not things. We can derive joy from things only up to a certain extent, and that too, as long as we have our loved ones around to share it with. But love transcends everything else. Quality time with family, friends, relatives and others who mean the world to us is an absolute necessity.

People over projects

Use things, not people. Love people, not things.

During the COVID-19 pandemic, we saw much fear in people, especially the fear of losing a loved one. I know a lady who was extremely worried about her husband repeatedly travelling to a different state during such unsure times. The husband, on the other hand, was an easy-going person. They were unable to understand each other; him, her overreaction and her, his unwillingness to listen to her. This led to an unfavourable environment. The communication was lost in transit: they failed to make their way to each other due to their unwillingness to understand each other's perspectives. I spoke to both of them and gave a few suggestions. I especially gave priority and attention to the emotionally sensitive party. Though the husband is very loving and caring, he has a different outlook than his wife when it comes to handling such situations. Maturity is of extreme essence here. In a relationship, it is not about right or wrong or who thinks what, but instead, just being there for each other, especially when they need us.

A few days later, I spoke to the wife again. She was still upset because her husband was travelling the next day. It was a desperate situation. However, the next morning, the wife called me and sounded extremely happy, She informed me that even though the husband had left as per his schedule, he had returned home from the airport. Thus he made a huge investment in their relationship. When our people need us, everything else, all other commitments, should take the back seat. The need to feel valued is, at its core, a very human trait, and when we make people feel loved, they will be more than happy to walk the extra mile to make us feel the same way when we need them.

It is not what we have but whom we have in life that matters. Things, projects and commitments will come and go but the time we spend with our loved ones is most precious and limited; it will not come back and let us not take them for granted.

Reconcile

'A happily ever after' is a fairy tale that is incompatible with the real world. An ideal relationship is not devoid of challenges. What matters is how we overcome them.

Familiarity breeds contempt. The more time we spend together, the more we get to know each other as well. As a result, we tend to take people for granted and focus on their shortcomings. We become complacent in our efforts to sustain the relationship compared to what we did to build it. We become less conscious of the continuous effort required to keep things going. It is as they say, 'A casual attitude leads to a casualty.' The relationship turns sour, and the people in that relationship become bitter. However, know that the choice to reconcile is always ours. The three As or reconciliation have proved fruitful.

Acknowledge

In relationships that have gone sour, we can introspect and ask others to give an unbiased opinion on whether we were wrong. The first step to mending anything is to acknowledge one's flaws.

Apologize

Just as harsh words hurt, humble words heal. We can take considerable steps in rebuilding relationships by apologizing. Only a tree laden with fruit bends low. So no harm in taking a lower position. In fact, when we do it, the other person's heart also softens. Apologizing does not come from a place of weakness but rather from wisdom and maturity. An admission of vulnerability can go a long way in fixing broken relationships.

Amend

Do everything possible to correct the consequences of your mistakes.

Communicate your needs

The other person is not God. They cannot be expected to read our minds. We cannot make assumptions based on some perception. Communication is the essence of all relationships. We must communicate how we feel in a gentle way. When a person is earnest about a relationship, they will, unfailingly, make efforts to do the needful on their part. Eventually, relationships are all about what the other person needs.

Forgive minor mistakes

No one is perfect. Hence, forgive minor mistakes. We do not have even a fraction of an idea about what the other person is going through. So, always be kind, be the bigger person and let things go. It does not take a great person to see faults in others. But it does take an exceptional person to see the good in the midst of the bad. Remember that only a humble and pure heart can forgive.

When someone is hard on you, it may have little to do with you.

Accept challenges

All relationships have problems. Our ability to overcome them defines our relationship's strength.

There will be tests. Expect loads of them. Life is equally bumpy for everyone on the ride. They are a part of growing together and, most importantly, part of the process. We must expect challenges and when they come, accept them and deal with them too.

A challenge in a relationship does not mean something is wrong. Simply put, it just means we need to address and resolve something that is not working in the relationship. It is a good reality check. But what it is not is a reason to terminate the relationship.

Appreciate

The need to feel valued and loved is innate. Be very generous in appreciating every small gesture of love or kindness and every little act of service. Be generous in praise.

And if you have to point out a fault, do it privately. Offer criticism with tenderness because people are fragile. This is true in any institutional setup, whether it is a family, society or corporates.

Spiritual foundation

A family that prays together, stays together.

Even though we are discussing this at the end, it is the most important of all principles and completely non-negotiable. By only applying this principle correctly, we will have the strength and intelligence to implement the rest.

A few years back, one of our senior devotees had a talk at MIT, Cambridge. At the end of his talk, a young man approached him and started conversing in Hindi, though he was not of Indian origin. Surprised, the devotee asked the young man how he knew Hindi. The young man replied that his extremely wealthy father had given him all luxuries in life. Once, he requested his father to give him something that he had not been able to give. It was the experience of a family life! The father told the man to visit India. He said the country was the only one of its kind where family culture is still prevalent. The young man came to

India and stayed with a family in Banaras for two years; thus, he learnt Hindi during his stay.

Despite so many obstacles, our country has maintained family culture even to this day. The sole credit for keeping us together must be attributed to our rich and spiritual culture. It is so powerful that it has become second nature to us.

When as a family, we regularly come together (even if it is just once a week for thirty–forty minutes) to hear and chant the holy name, fame, qualities and pastimes of the Lord, to worship Him, to serve Him, a very potent energy descends from the spiritual realm and binds us together.

We want to live, and live happily ever after. This is certainly possible but only if we create a powerful spiritual environment at home with Lord Krishna as the focal point. If we can do this, we will not be separated from each other ever and can even be reunited in the spiritual realm to live happily forever.

IN A NUTSHELL

A baseless brawl, words are swallowed.
A bloated bottle, feelings float at its brim with sorrow.
Ensuring the relationship to dig its hollow.
Replaced communication with this bottle,
The silence drove my partner to throttle.
I, me, mine, craving the centre of attention every time.
The Lord reprimands this false ego to be a crime.
To love means to serve, it's the doorway to happiness, just observe.
Acknowledge, apologize, amend, save your relationship or it'll rend.
Think about each other's happiness, nip in the bud the fights of cattiness.

CHAPTER 3

EXPECTATIONS: HOW MUCH IS TOO MUCH?

The root cause of anxiety is endless expectations.

—His Holiness Radhanath Swami*

Once a monk and his beloved disciple were on their way to a spiritual journey. They saw a young princess waiting beside her royal palanquin, looking concerned. On enquiring, they learned that she was returning from a nearby kingdom and was in a hurry to reach the palace to attend a ceremonial event. However, exhausted by the tedious journey, her attendants could not bear to carry her further and thus requested to take some rest. The princess, however, felt

* Swami, Radhanath, Twitter post, 22 October 2012, 2.28 p.m., https://twitter.com/radhanathswami/status/260304110027415553

somewhat agitated hearing this. The monk decided to offer help, and he and his disciple carried the princess in her palanquin for a considerable distance. This act of generosity allowed her attendants to refresh themselves in the meantime. Once the attendants undertook the remaining journey, the two monks bowed in reverence and decided to walk away. The princess waved them off without expressing any form of gratitude. Vexed by such an atrocious display, the disciple fumed inside. He expected his guru to react. To his surprise, the guru's face reflected a strange silence, an incredible calmness. Unable to embrace this silence, the disciple blurted out in resentment, 'That Princess needs to learn some manners. She could have been a little appreciative of our help.'

The guru smiled gently and said, 'Our disappointment is a result of our over-expectations.' The disciple was not convinced. He replied, 'We carried her for such a long distance; she could have at least smiled back. A smile would have cost her nothing. I genuinely feel annoyed; after all, we carried her for so long!'

The guru replied, 'I set that palanquin down hours ago, so why are you still carrying the burden?'

It is human nature to expect rewards from our investments, whether in relationships, careers or any other aspect of life. In a way, expectations can be helpful: they give us a sense of motivation and direction or help us meet certain standards. However, when expectations influence our thoughts too much or when we give in to others' wishes instead of following our own path, it can significantly affect our well-being.

We expect a lot from ourselves and others. Unfortunately, our expectations are often unrealistic and cause of stress and self-criticism. So how do we manage expectations instead of letting them rule our lives? Should we not expect at all?

Speaking from an absolute perspective, the answer is yes! In the Bhagavad Gita [2.47], Lord Krishna teaches

karmany evadhikaras te
ma phalesu kadachana
ma karma-phala-hetur bhur
ma te sango 'stv akarmani

(You have a right to perform your prescribed duty but you are not entitled to the fruits of action. Never consider yourself to be the cause of the results of your activities, and never be attached to not doing your duty.)

We must simply focus on being and doing our best, knowing well that apart from our best intentions and endeavour, nothing is in our control. Expecting nothing in return will avoid future disappointments.

Nonetheless, we know that we are not that evolved to be completely detached. We do so much for someone and can't we expect even a 'little' from them? At least a little act of kindness or a few words of acknowledgment?

We can, but we must have realistic expectations. We must understand others' and our limitations and, thus, acknowledge that everyone is an individual and has their own nature, priorities and thought patterns.

WHY DO WE HAVE EXPECTATIONS?

Because we want to feel complete.

'Ananda-mayo "bhyasat"' (Vedanta-sutra 1.1.12).

(The soul, by nature, is pleasure-seeking or after happiness.)

We are parts and parcels of God, the supreme source. When we become disconnected from our source, the source of all happiness, that is, Lord Krishna or God who is spiritual, we feel incomplete. To complete ourselves, we endeavour to find the missing link in different objects, situations or people of this world. Thus the expectations.

As we are spiritual by nature, a spiritual being trying to find happiness in something material is an incompatible situation.

On this earth, everything has a shelf life. In other words, everything in the world is temporary, and so our quest never ends.

WHAT ARE EXPECTATIONS?

Expectations are 'premeditated resentments'.

The word 'premeditated' is often used in cricket, such as 'the premeditated cricket shot'. It means that even before the bowler has bowled the ball, the batsman has decided on a particular shot he is going to play. This often gets the batsman into trouble and eventually gets him out because the bowler might be thinking differently. When our expectations do not match our reality, we face problems.

Expectations are what we think will happen, while reality is what transpires. Though we hope these two will be the same, often, they are not. This disparity of expectations versus reality can lead to feelings of discontentment and unhappiness. Invariably we resent the person who fails to fulfil our expectations or we feel helpless and angry.

THE DANGER

When our expectations outmatch our reality, it often means we do not appreciate what we have. Instead, we compare what we have to what we could have. For example, one study found that participants who were exposed to a subliminal reminder of wealth spent less time savouring a chocolate bar and exhibited less enjoyment of the experience than other subjects who were not reminded of wealth.

SOME UNREALISTIC EXPECTATIONS

Realistic expectations are healthy and inspire courage and dedication towards a goal. Unrealistic ones (which can never be fulfilled)—such as, everyone should like or love me, everyone should behave the way I want, my life should be problem free, I should be successful in whatever I do—can make life miserable. Having too many expectations causes constant anxiety, misunderstanding and if not met, it can kill.

On a cold winter night, a king once met a poor old man outside his palace. He asked him, 'Don't you feel cold as you are not wearing any coat?' The old man replied, 'I don't have one but I am used to this. I have been bearing this cold weather for many years and now I have developed the strength to live through it every year, by God's grace.' On hearing this, the king said, 'Wait for me. I will bring you one.' The poor man was happy to hear this and agreed to wait for the king.

When the king entered his palace, he got busy with his duties and forgot about the poor man. The next morning when the soldiers came out, they saw the cold, stricken body of the old man with a message written on the ground, 'Long live the king. I had been living through these cold winters easily all this while but last night, your promise to get me a blanket took away my life.'

WHAT DO WE DO NOW?

Human beings have emotions and, more than anything else, need love and affection from others to survive. Thus expectations cannot completely vanish from our hearts. But the reality must not be forgotten either. Here are some principles that can help us navigate the realm of expectations.

Communicate clearly

Unspoken expectations are almost guaranteed to go unfulfilled. Talking openly about what we expect from the other person might improve our chances of fulfilment. Communicate your needs gently. Each person is unique. Some are very sensitive and some are extremely carefree. The sensitive one might need an explicit expression of affection from others but the other person might have an entirely opposite personality. The person could be a well-wisher at the same time but may not understand our needs. In all cases, let us not assume that just because we are close to a person, they are aware of our needs. At the same time, it is unrealistic to think that merely communicating our expectations clearly will get people to behave as we want them to. But without communicating, there is no chance at all.

Do not expect the same level of intimacy in every relationship

One of the biggest mistakes or illusions is to expect the same kind of experience in every relationship: husband, wife, friends, family, relatives, colleagues and society. Not all relationships are the same, so the level of commitment, intimacy and tolerance will differ. Accepting the reality will reduce our pain by almost 70–80 per cent. With some, we could be close, while with others, we could just do the needful. Accept the fact that the same kind of intimacy will not exist in every relationship.

Learn to accept others as they are

Accept the reality that everybody is different and fighting their own battle. Learning to accept people the way they are opens a whole new dimension of peace. Instead of feeling miserable, we enjoy the variety that is present in the world. God has made everyone a unique individual. Not even identical twins are the same. Accept and respect everyone for who they are. After all, why should someone try to live their life our way? Would we ourselves ever do the same?

Focus on what is within control

The only thing within our control is our actions, behaviour, growth and response to various events in life. Lord Krishna in the Bhagavad Gita [2.47] says:

karmanye vadhikaraste,
ma phaleshou kada chana,
ma karma phala hetur bhurmatey
sangostva akarmani

Do your duty but be detached from the result. Why should one do so? Because the result will follow its own course as destiny is also a big player. Hence, focusing on the effort and our duties (things we can control) will save us from unwarranted stress.

Lower your expectations

Expecting less from others or ourselves can provide immediate relief. There will always be people who will criticize us but there will also be people who praise us; there will be people who give us happiness and there will be people who will make us sad; there will be times when we will earn a profit, and there will be times when we will lose. The idea of leading a good life is to understand that the world is full of such dualities, and there will be times when our expectations will differ from reality.

Keep a variety of options ready

Sometimes expectations only focus on one outcome, and when it is not met, we feel disappointed. Usually, there are several ways to achieve a goal. We must try to find new ways to fulfil our wishes.

Keep investing

The Lord has created this universe in such a way that if we do good to others, goodness will be returned to us and if we hurt others, that pain will also come back to us. Hence, one should continue investing well even if we do not get back as returns from the same person. The problem is that we expect returns from the person in whose life we have invested. And when we do not get what we want, we feel disappointed. The law of karma is that if we do good to someone, that goodness will come back to us, though it may not necessarily be from the same source. If we hurt someone, the other person may not be able to hurt us back. But the pain we have caused someone will undoubtedly come back to us from a source which is in a position to hurt us. So we must keep up the good work even if we do not see immediate results.

We do good because we are good. The way we treat others is a statement about us. And the way others treat us is a statement about them.

Address the eternal cause

The Bhagavad Gita explains, 'We are not these material bodies, but spiritual beings'. Love, affection and reciprocation are needs of the soul and not of the body. The body is dead matter and the soul is spiritual. No amount of matter or material acquisition can bring satisfaction to us. A spiritual being trying to find happiness in the matter is an incompatible situation. We may put great effort into satisfying the body, but our real identity is different from that of the body.

For example, if I am hungry, I cannot ask my friend to eat on my behalf as that will not satisfy my hunger. Similarly, just providing for the body does not guarantee nourishment to us. We are different from the body. If we seek pleasure, we have to do so in things that are of a similar nature, that is, spiritual. God is spiritual and His name, fame, qualities and service are spiritual. When we connect with Him through His devotional service, beginning with hearing and chanting about Him in the association of His dear devotees, we truly start experiencing contentment within and stop expecting the same from the outside world.

George Harrison became world famous and earned extraordinary wealth at a very early age. On his visit to India, he looked at a monk walking on the streets and said, 'I want to be like him. With all this wealth and fame, I am still not satisfied. Look at the monk's face; he has something I do not have'. Thus, if we deeply connect to our spiritual self, that is, our true self, by connecting to our source (Lord Krishna) and chanting His names (such as the Hare Krishna mahamantra), worshipping Him, remembering Him, associating with devotees, hearing from scriptures like the Bhagavad Gita and Shrimad Bhagavatam regularly, then we shall experience such deep satisfaction that we will not be bothered by anything, whether we have everything or nothing. We will not feel the need for validation by others and we will not hanker for anything because we are already fulfilled.

The tenth canto of Shrimad Bhagavatam explains, 'Whenever Krishna had to take His lunch, He would sit down, along with His elder brother Balarama, on the banks of river Yamuna in Vrindavan. Both the brothers would sit in the middle, and all the boys would sit around them in a circle. Krishna knew everyone's need to feel loved and cared for. Thus, He would have his mystical potency expand in such a way that each cowherd boy would think that Krishna was looking at him and him only. Each boy wanted Krishna's exclusive attention, and He knew it. Even the boys sitting behind him would feel Krishna looking at them only.' Thus Krishna fulfilled everyone's expectations. Only the Lord can truly reciprocate our longings and fulfil them.

As Lord Krishna says in the Bhagavad Gita [2.59],

vishaya vinivartante
niraharasya dehinah
rasa-varjam raso 'py asya
param dristva nivartate

(The embodied soul may be restricted from sense enjoyment, though the taste for sense objects remains. But, ceasing such engagements by experiencing a higher taste, he is fixed in consciousness.)

One cannot give up the lower taste unless one gains some higher taste. Instead of just struggling with our expectations, we should recognize and acknowledge the eternal cause and try and take care of it.

All solutions discussed so far except the last one are temporary solutions. They will help you immediately but only to a certain extent. On the other hand, connecting to our true spiritual self by connecting with God is a permanent solution. By connecting to our real spiritual nature, we will always feel content and not be bothered by the endless expectations.

IN A NUTSHELL

Disappointments devise distressed dents in the mind.

Unfulfilled expectations evoke exasperated disappointments in life.

Expecting extolled, but alas, the situation was not in your hold.

Expecting gold, but it was only a plastic mould.

Expecting obedience, but it was only dire deviance.

Expecting a remarkable reaction, in hand an irrelevant interaction.

In order to seek happiness approach holiness.

Let Godliness complete you as a means to repel emptiness.

The divine's fulfilment wipes the slate clean of expectations with excessiveness.

Grasp acceptingness, put an end to anxiousness, live a life of blissfulness.

CHAPTER 4

FORGIVENESS: WHERE TO DRAW A LINE?

> To forgive is to set a prisoner free and discover that the prisoner was you.
>
> —Lewis B. Smedes*

Forgive and forget is a piece of advice that every counsellor or life coach gives to individuals who want to come out of bitter memories. But most people find it difficult to forgive as it is notoriously difficult. It is easier said than done. Forgiveness seems to be a lovely idea until we have a situation where we ourselves need to forgive.

When someone has done damage that appears at the time to be irreconcilable, we are filled with anger and bitterness towards the person. Instead of forgetting it and moving forward

* *Forgive and Forget: Healing the Hurts We Don't Deserve* (HarperOne, 2007).

in life, many of us keep a running score and hold what we like to call a grudge. Holding a grudge is like carrying around a heavy dead body full of maggots. It does not harm the person to whom the grudge is directed; it infects the person carrying this burden.

However, mastering the art of forgiveness plays a crucial role in happiness and the quality of our life.

Anyone who has suffered a grievous hurt knows that when our inner world is badly disrupted, it is difficult to concentrate on anything other than our turmoil to avenge the pain. And when we hold on to hurt, we are emotionally broken and our relationships suffer.

WHAT IS FORGIVENESS?

Forgiveness is a conscious, deliberate and voluntary decision to release feelings of resentment or vengeance towards a person or group who have harmed us, regardless of whether they actually deserve it or not.

In simple words, forgiveness is developing compassion and accepting others for being imperfect, while at the same time honouring our boundaries and protecting ourselves. It is about freeing oneself from our own negative 'victim' story of what we believed happened to us.

We have heard that we cannot make someone forgive us. However even more difficult is to make ourselves forgive someone.

Forgiveness is a process and sometimes an elusive one. But certainly not impossible.

Two monks were washing their bowls in the river when they noticed a scorpion drowning. One monk immediately scooped it up and set it upon the bank. In the process, he was stung. He returned to washing the bowl when he noticed the scorpion fall into the water again. The monk saved the scorpion and was stung again.

The other monk asked, 'My dear friend, why do you continue to save the scorpion when you know its nature is to sting.'

'Because,' the monk replied, 'to save it is my nature.'

FORGIVENESS: WHY?

The quality of forgiveness is very important for our peace of mind and any peace and harmony within this world. The reasons are as follows.

The four defects

All humans are born with four defects: (i) imperfect senses, (ii) tendency to cheat, (iii) tendency to commit mistakes, and (iv) tendency to fall under an illusion. Thus no matter how much we try to seek perfection in others, it will not be possible. We are not perfect, then how can we have such expectations from others? If we wish to be forgiven when we make a mistake, we must learn to forgive others too.

The age of kali yuga

We live in kali yuga, which means '*kalah pradhaan yug*,' that is, the age of quarrel and hypocrisy. The environment is surcharged with these for no concrete reasons. In the age of kali yuga, those with the best intentions commit mistakes as they are affected by the environment around them. So it is important to be lenient with everyone. Relationships, communities and countries cannot survive without developing the quality of forgiveness.

The power of time

Time deteriorates everything. With time, things perish. The world functions under specific laws. One of the laws is the law of gravity, which means whatever goes up, must come down in due course of time. For instance, if a structural engineer is building something, he must work against this law of gravity. The structure has the tendency to collapse, but he needs to ensure the structure does not, by working against the law of gravity despite the impediments. Similarly, in today's day and age, there are so many stimulants in this world to drag everything down, especially our consciousness and our relationships. Understanding this aspect of the world we live in, the practice of the quality of forgiveness becomes essential.

For peace

Forgiveness is to be practiced for our own benefit. Hatred, resentment, and vengeance affect our hearts. When someone hurts us, we are angry as we feel our rights have been violated.

His Holiness Radhanath Swami says, 'Not forgiving is like picking up a piece of burning hot charcoal and holding on to it day after day, week after week, year after year with the intention of throwing it on the object of our abuse'. But who has suffered for all these years? The person who holds it. If we keep this blazing fire of hatred towards others in our hearts and do not forgive, it will burn to ashes all our virtues and spiritual inclinations and even burn all those around us.

THE ART OF FORGIVENESS: HOW TO FORGIVE?

It is not easy, but the benefits of forgiving and forgetting surpass the pain of holding on to a grudge. Here are a few tips to make peace with others and move on.

Let us be kind to ourselves

Do not punish yourself for someone else's mistakes. Remember that it is in our best interest to forgive people. By carrying the baggage of revenge and bad memories for a long time, we forget that it is stealing our peace of mind. By having negativity in mind, we cannot have good physical health. There are physical manifestations of negative emotions in our body. Toxic and destructive emotions have the potential to activate certain diseases if we do not attend to our emotional well-being. The person who has hurt us must be living in his own world and enjoying life. He must have even forgotten that anything went wrong between us and them. But, we are carrying that grudge and punishing ourselves. The weak can never forgive. Forgiveness is the attribute of the strong.

Put yourself in the shoes of the wrongdoer

Most likely, that person has some history whereby they were mistreated and lied to, or they may even have some physiological pathology that leads them down the wrong path. Love, honesty and kindness come from a pure heart and hatred, deceit and evil come from a dark and damaged heart. Try to sympathize with the evil-doer and their sickness, and while this does not correct what they have done, it takes away the feeling that their actions were personally directed at you. Even if we cannot understand why someone behaved in a particular way, we must try to recognize the feelings or experiences that triggered their hurtful behaviour.

Replace the 'victim story'

Sometimes we have a longstanding 'victim story' that we constantly repeat to ourselves and others. It typically describes how we have been victimized, and someone ruined our life. We believe it was not our mistake and convince ourselves and others that we are the victims.

We need to change our story. It is not true that someone has victimized us. Yes! Someone's actions did pain us. But, it is we who did not respond or handle it well. Let us come out of that victim mindset and focus on what we did to recover from or cope with the situation. By shifting from 'poor me' to 'here's what I did', we no longer cast ourselves as a victim and it becomes easier to forget and forgive.

Lower the expectations

Start giving lesser importance to people and situations. Do not get hurt easily; reduce your expectations from others. Even we are not able to live up to everyone's expectations every time.

It is not necessary that the person on the opposite side will give the same importance to you in their life. Do not give the remote of your mental peace to others. When we expect less, we get hurt less.

However, forgiveness will not necessarily erase all our pain. When somebody has deliberately betrayed us, and something reminds us about what that person has done, it is natural to feel hurt or resentment or even spasms of hate.

Forgiveness does not mean we lose all negative feelings forever. But it does mean that the hurt no longer occupies the centre stage in our life.

Learn from the experience: sometimes we win, sometimes we learn

If a business partner has taken advantage of you, ask yourself: how did I get into such a position. Be aware of this and apply it to your future endeavours. Similarly, in a relationship, if we ignore the red flags, tolerate intolerable behaviour, or somehow set ourselves up for this incident to happen, take note of it. We have to ensure that it is not repeated. Be proactive in dealing with similar situations or get out of the relationship before you become a victim again. The incident should act as a learning for the future. Consider the treachery as a service that will help you dodge a bigger bullet in the future.

Forgive but do not trust

If someone hurts us, intentionally or unintentionally and has done it for the first time, we should immediately forgive, for our peace and for the sake of the relationship. On the other hand, if someone is a serial offender, we may choose to forgive. But, forgiveness should never be at the cost of trust, that is, you may forgive, but you should not trust the person and maintain a respectful distance. As they say, 'If you cheat me once, shame on you; if you cheat me twice, shame on me'.

Confront the offender

At times it may be important to confront the individual who is repeatedly causing pain to make them understand that there is a line that they cannot keep crossing. It could be communicated in a gentle yet firm manner. If this is at the cost of the relationship, it is fine as this shows that the other person is not serious about the same and thus not mature enough to understand or invest in it.

Draw a line and let the person know

Once, Sage Narada visited a village where he noticed the children fearful of a snake living close by. So, Sage Narada visited the snake and asked him not to scare the children. As Sage Narada was a divine being, the snake agreed to his request. When the sage visited the village again, he noticed that the snake was scared this time. On enquiring from the snake about its miserable state, Sage Narada learned that on his request, the snake had stopped troubling the children. However, the children had begun troubling him, throwing stones and beating him with sticks. Sage Narada told the snake, 'I asked you not to bite but did not ask you not to hiss to scare them away. You may not bite, but you can act as if you will bite.'

This is something we also need to practice in life. To draw a line and let the other person know , 'Dear Sir! I respect you and am always ready to help you if you do not cross this line. This is important to prevent the other person from repeating the offence and disrupting our peace.

View our inability to forgive as the impurity of our own heart

By nature, the soul is pure. Hence, the quality of forgiveness is also innate in us. Our spiritual nature is covered with layers of impurities from many lifetimes, and the inability to forgive and hold on to a grudge is the result of that. Instead of blaming the offender and making the offender the focus of our lives, we should take it as a reminder of the impurities within our own heart and work on improving and purifying it. How? As Shri Chaitanya-charitamrita, Madhya-lila [22.107] says,

nitya-siddha krishna-prema 'sadhya' kabhu nàya
shravanadi-shuddha-chitte karaye daya

(Pure love for Krishna is eternally established in the hearts of the living entities. It is not something to be gained from another source. When the heart is purified by hearing and chanting, this love naturally awakens.)

When we hear and chant about the glories of the Lord, the heart gradually gets purified. The more the heart gets purified, the easier it becomes to practice forgiveness. So if the heart is completely purified and there is no anger within, there is no possibility of anger manifesting without.

Pray for the offender

This solution is the most difficult to implement as it requires a very evolved consciousness. We grow when we help and pray for the growth of others instead of blaspheming them. If someone exhibits anger, greed, envy, pride or illusion, we must understand that it is a disease.

For instance, upon seeing somebody coughing, bleeding or vomiting in a hospital, we do not get angry because we understand they are patients. A patient will be in pain because he is suffering from some disease. Similarly, when someone is hurting or misbehaving, we should understand that he is suffering from the disease of the heart called anger and envy. Hence, it is important that we rise above and not behave like a victim but see the other person with much compassion.

Once Draupadi told Yudhishthira to take revenge on Duryodhana as he had inflicted a lot of injustice on the five brothers. Yudhishthira replied, 'If we also behave the same way as Duryodhana, then there is no difference between him and us. The best response to him will be for us to forgive him.'

View the other person as an instrument of your karma

Whatever situation in life we are in today, is because of our karma. Srila Prabhupada once said, 'Never be angry with the instrument of your karma.'*

Acceptance is the key. Learn to accept your karma. If you do so, 70 per cent of your pain will vanish. View such situations as an opportunity to grow, as if someone is showing you the mirror to understand your shortcomings and to work on the same. Do not retaliate against the instruments of your karma as that will implicate you further. Instead think of how we can nullify your karma.

---

* ISKON Desire Tree, 'Srila Prabhupada Quotes on Forgiveness', blog, 17 October 2020.

In Sri Brahma-samhita [5.24], Lord Brahma says karma can only be nullified through the process of devotional service (bhakti):

yas tv indragopam athavendram aho sva-karma-
bandhanurupa-phala-bhajanam atanoti
karmani nirdahati kintu ca bhakti-bhajam
govindam adi-purusam tam aham bhajami

(I adore the primeval Lord Govinda, who burns up to their roots all fruitive activities of those who are imbued with devotion and impartially ordains for each the due enjoyment of the fruits of one's activities, of all those who walk in the path of work, under the chain of their previously performed works, no less in the case of the tiny insect that bears the name of indragopa than in that of Indra, the king of the devas.)

Forgive to be forgiven

As you sow, so shall you reap. Hence, we must forgive others so that we can be forgiven too when we are on the wrong side. What goes around must come around.

Raise yourselves spiritually

The material platform is the duality platform where we constantly oscillate between happiness and distress, honour and dishonour, praise and criticism, and so on. As long as we stay on this platform, we shall continue to be affected. Thus we must raise ourselves to a spiritual platform, the platform of equality where forgiveness becomes our nature, and we do not even need to make an effort to forgive. We will not even feel that an offense has been committed.

A beautiful episode is described in Shrimad Bhagavatam, Canto 9, which illustrates this point beautifully. Once there was a great king by the name of Ambarisha. He was the emperor of the planet in the dynasty of Lord Rama and a pure devotee of Lord Vishnu. He had surrendered everything to the Lord, and despite having the kingdom, the family and many other responsibilities, his priority in life was devotional service to the Lord. Due to this, the Lord was so pleased with him that He had deputed His ultimate weapon, the Sudarshan Chakra, to King Ambarisha's kingdom for his protection.

One day the great Sage Durvasa came to see the king when he was about to break his Ekadashi fast in Madhuvan, one of the twelve forests of Vrindavan. As a guest had arrived, the king invited the sage to eat first. Sage Durvasa was known for his eccentric temper. Instead of sitting down to eat, he chose to bathe first. While doing so, he went into deep meditation. King Ambarisha was in a dilemma. He wondered how to break his fast without his guest being served first. His fast was his service to the Lord and thus extremely important. He consulted a few brahmin priests on the matter. They suggested that he drank a few drops of water, which was equivalent to eating and not eating as well. King Ambarisha followed the advice and drank a few drops of water. After some time, Sage Durvasa returned. He saw King Ambarisha humbly standing and waiting for him. Through his mystic powers, the sage learned that the king had drunk a few drops of water. He got furious thinking that the king had transgressed the etiquette. In great anger, he ripped a bunch of hair from his head and threw it on the ground. Instantly a fiery demon appeared at the scene and moved towards the king to attack him. But King Ambarisha remained undisturbed and stood there with his hands folded. Just then, the Lord's Sudarshan chakra, dazzling, effulgent as millions of suns rising simultaneously, appeared on the scene to shield the king.

The Sudarshan chakra destroyed the fiery demon and then moved dangerously towards Sage Durvasa, the main offender. Sage Durvasa ran as fast as he could until he reached Lord Brahma's planet. When Lord Brahma saw the chakra, he advised the sage to run further as the chakra would also destroy his abode. Then the sage ran to Lord Shiva, and Lord Shiva also did not entertain his request, on seeing the might of the Sudarshan chakra. As his last resort, the sage finally went to Vaikuntha, where Lord Vishnu resided and fell at his feet, requesting the Lord to protect him from His powerful weapon. Lord Vishnu politely declined and said, 'Even I do not have the power to forgive you. My devotees are my heart. They know no one but me and I know no one but them. And how can I give up the association of such devotees who have given up everything for my sake. Any offence towards me can be easily forgiven, but any offence towards my devotees can only be forgiven by my devotees. So, unless King Ambarisha forgives you, even I cannot forgive you and save you from the Sudarshan chakra.'

After travelling for one whole year trying to seek protection, when the sage returned to King Ambarisha, he found him standing at the same place with his hands joined, waiting for his guest to eat first. Sage Durvasa fell at King Ambarisha's feet and begged for forgiveness. The king, as noble a soul as he was, felt embarrassed that such a great sage was asking for his forgiveness. The king also felt guilty that the sage had to suffer so much because of him. The thought never passed him that the sage had tried to kill him. No offense had been committed at all, according to him. Thus, on the sage's insistence, he forgave him immediately, and the Sudarshan chakra also calmed down.

This is true forgiveness, where we do not even think an offense has been committed. However, such a platform can only be reached by regularly engaging in the devotional service of the Lord and chanting daily: the Hare Krishna mahamantra. We should also study the Bhagavad Gita, Shrimad Bhagavatam, and worship the deities such as Radha–Krishna, Sita–Ram or Laxmi–Narayan, offer prayers and worship Tulasi(the sacred plant dear to Lord Krishna) in the association of the devotees.

This is a permanent solution. As long as we stay on the material platform, there will be problems. However, when we rise above the spiritual platform, anything happening on a lower platform does not affect us.

Real forgiveness must come from the heart. In the beginning, we may forgive on a more superficial platform. If it has been a traumatic experience, forgiving may take a long time. But we should have that mindset to forgive. We should have that prayer. Krishna is bhavagrahi. He understands our intentions and progress, even if we do not have the power or the ability to do it. According to the Bhagavad Gita [9.22],

ananyash chintayanto mam
ye janah paryupasate
tesham nityabhiyuktanam
yoga-kshemam vahamy aham

(But those who always worship Me with exclusive devotion, meditating on My transcendental form, to them I carry what they lack, and I preserve what they have.)

In the Bhagavad Gita, Lord Krishna teaches us that when we aspire to surrender to Him and take shelter in Him, He preserves what we have and carries what we lack. On our own, it is impossible. Impossible to even remember the above-mentioned solutions. We never have the power to forgive. But we know it is a right. By forgiving, we will be relieved of the poison of hatred. We know it will be pleasing before God. Therefore, we do not try to inflict the same pain on that person. Instead we pray to be relieved of this disease. We pray to God for that power, and we go to saintly people and reveal our hearts to them and ask for their help. We try to cleanse our hearts through prayer, chanting God's names and meditating on the Lord. And if we continue in this way, understanding our intention, Lord Krishna will surely help us.

IN A NUTSHELL

One contender in this race, requiring a constant pace, presuming that is the only way.
A bulky burden on her back, not cutting any slack, fanning the flames of her decay.
She turns around to heed the audience yell out loud,
'Does holding grudges make you proud?'
No, but it's vital. Forgiveness is a never-ending spiral.
An unforgiving girl in this race, competing for some peace of mind.
Overburdened by her grudges, she knows it's time to leave it behind.
Opening her arms to the Lord, learning to forgive and mending the chord.
Accepting that everything is healed with time, another's mistake not worth a dime.
Forgiveness for peace, forgiveness for self, forgiveness to get rid of vain stress.

CHAPTER 5

LET GO, LIVE FREE

Once there was a free bird. Like many other birds, she flew in the sky, caught midges for lunch and swam in the summer rain trickles.

But she had a habit: every time some event occurred in her life, whether good or bad, the bird picked up a stone from the ground. Every day she sorted out her stones, laughed remembering joyful events and cried remembering the sad ones.

The bird always took the stones with her. Whether she was flying in the sky or walking on the earth, she never forgot about them. The years passed and the free bird had many stones. She still sorted them and remembered the past. It was becoming increasingly difficult to fly, and one day it could not fly anymore.

The once free bird could not walk on Earth. She was unable to make a move on her own. She could not catch midges anymore; only rare rain gave her the necessary moisture. But the bird bravely endured all the hardships and guarded her precious memories.

After some time, the bird died of starvation and thirst. And only a pitiful bunch of worthless stones remained with her for a long time.

The story teaches an important and pertinent lesson:

We will have to let all our anger and hurt go when we die, so we may as well release them beforehand. Whenever we die, our consciousness goes along with us. Why carry the baggage to the next life and spoil a fresh start? Why spend our entire life like the bird in bondage when we can live free? Why deprive ourselves of the opportunity to live and enjoy the life we have been blessed with? Whatever has happened has happened. Let go of it!

THE HURT

We usually tend to get hurt when someone criticizes us, ignores us, abandons us or lets us down.

The feeling of hurt has the potential to stay with us forever and leave scars on our hearts. It can result in a prolonged infection of the mind if not dealt with efficiently.

And let us not have the unrealistic expectation that others will fix our pain. It will simply put us in a weaker position.

While somebody can guide and inspire us, we are the ones who must fix ourselves. And this is the most challenging thing to accept.

THE PAIN BODY

We have something called a 'pain body', a collection of all our hurts, sorrows anger and fears. This creates an energetic field around our physical bodies, which we carry everywhere with us like baggage.

This pain body needs more and more pain to expand. So, when some untoward incident happens, a spontaneous reaction inflicts further pain upon us, and this pain body continues to expand. The cumulative effect of such a painful body is disastrous.

We tend to keep collecting more and more hurt (like the bird collecting stones as in the story above) and make ourselves appear bigger victims. And experience states that once people go into this negative shell, after a certain point, they start experiencing some pleasure in being a victim, unwilling to come out. Just like a camel which eats thorns and begins to enjoy his own blood due to its tongue bleeding, not realizing it is hurting itself.

THE MEANING OF 'LET GO'

It feels good to let go—not when other people tell us to 'let go and move on', but when we see the necessity of it. Letting go does not mean forgetting or whitewashing the other person's behaviour. It means protecting ourselves from the corrosive effects of staying stuck.

Chronic anger and bitterness dissipate our energy and sap our creativity. Each of us has a certain amount of energy that fuels our spirit.

If anger keeps us stuck in the past, we will neither be fully in the present nor can we move forward into the future. We do not need to forgive a particular bad action when the other person fails to genuinely acknowledge the wrong. But we do need, over time, to dissipate its emotional charge. We need to accept the reality that sometimes the wrongdoer is unreachable and unrepentant, and it is our choice to carry the wrongdoing on our shoulders or let it go. We can either punish 'ourselves' for someone else's wrongdoing or understand it is their disease, and focus on our growth instead.

A BIG RELIEF AWAITS US

Just as putting aside weights offers physical relief, putting aside grudges offers emotional relief. However, our mind viscerally opposes the idea of letting go, 'This person has hurt me so much. How can I just let them go scot-free?'

Letting go of grudges does not necessarily mean letting others go scot-free; it essentially means letting ourselves go free. In essence, we do not want to suffer for what has already happened and something that is beyond our control. Peace manifests when we focus our energy on things we can control.

We now have to let go of the past; our false self, old self, ego; attachment to memories; fear, even the fear of letting go; guilt; blame; shame; the label of being adopted; doubt; and other people's opinions or judgements or our own judgements about ourselves.

We must be willing to let go of the life we have planned to live the life waiting for us.

HOW TO LET GO?

It is a question many of us ask ourselves or other each time we experience heartache or emotional pain.

One thing that connects us as human beings is our ability to feel pain. Whether that pain is physical or emotional, we all have experiences of being hurt. What separates us, though, is how we deal with that pain.

Once, a sage visited a king who was highly restless despite being surrounded by all types of luxuries. He kept on repeating, 'O venerable sage? Maya (illusion) has caught me. Please save me. I am suffering'.

The sage smiled and suddenly ran out of the palace with great speed and held on to a tree shouting, 'O tree! Please leave me. Please leave me!'

The king was shocked. He asked, 'What kind of behaviour is this? You are holding the tree and not vice versa. And you are shouting, "Leave me?" It is you who needs to let go of the tree'.

The sage turned to the king and calmly replied, 'Exactly, dear king. Just like it is I who am attached to the tree and not the other way around, we are the ones holding onto maya (illusion), and not her. We need to make a conscious effort to let go of her and thus lead a peaceful life'.

Similarly, holding on to the past can be a conscious decision, just like letting go and moving forward can be one.

The Lord has blessed every human being with something called 'free will'. In every situation and moment of life, we have the free will to respond.

Now that we have analysed the nature of the problem at hand, let us focus on the most critical part: the ways to deal with it!

Focus on the valuable lesson

We never fail. Sometimes we win, and sometimes we learn. When emotional pain prevents us from healing from a situation, it is a sign that we are not moving forward in a growth-oriented way. We are stuck. One of the best ways to heal from a hurt is to learn lessons from the situation and use those to focus on growth and forward momentum. If we get stuck thinking about what 'should have been', we can get obsessed with painful feelings and memories.

For example, If someone cheats on us, instead of simply lamenting, we can use the incident to learn to be careful in the future and not trust anyone so quickly.

Focus on the best option

If we wish to remain positive in all situations, we must always think, 'All right! This has happened now. I cannot undo it. But what is the "best" thing that I can do in this situation?' Just focus and do that.

Example one: Recently, the world was hit by the COVID-19 pandemic. We could not control or undo it. Some people became depressed, some complained, while others were angry. But many remained peaceful and even grateful—knowing they could do nothing to reverse it, they simply focussed on utilizing these moments to do what best could be done in the situation: spend time with the family, learn new skills, connect globally and spiritually. The situation was the same for everyone, but how people responded decided their level of happiness and misery.

Example two: When someone passes away, people grieve. But simply crying does not help the affected party or the soul that has passed away. We must focus on doing something that will help the soul's journey. Chanting the Bhagavad Gita, reciting Shrimad Bhagavatam, and chanting Krishna's holy names will help the departed soul and give a lot of positivity and inner strength to the people left behind.

If we focus on the unchangeable, we will simply get frustrated. Instead if we choose to concentrate our energy on the better options available that we can control, we shall experience peace.

See them as patients

We can either be a victim or an example/a healer. We must mentally keep ourselves in a higher position and not succumb to the negativity that others expose us to. Be compassionate. Feel pity. Pray for them. We might have to keep our distance from some people who have the habit of hurting us, but we need to look at them with much empathy. We may keep boundaries, but at the same time, we pray for them and ourselves.

Hate the sin. Not the sinner.

Affirmations

Everything begins with a thought. When someone abuses us, our mind begins to paralyse us through toxic thoughts. Thoughts, not people or situations, cause emotions in us. So if we can simply replace those thoughts with positive ones, we will not experience the pain.

Negative thoughts may enter our mind if we encounter a person who reminds us of a bad experience. Even though the individual may be standing ten feet away and doing no harm to us, our mind may start thinking negatively as we are carrying the baggage of the 'pain body'. To counteract this situation, affirm the following, 'Everyone is nice, everyone is loving, everyone is caring. I am fine.' Repeat it five or six times.

Immediately we shall experience a surcharge of positivity within us. Whatever our mind hears, again and again, it starts accepting. And the reason? We have simply understood the real cause of hurt (our thought patterns) and we have found a way to change them.

Do not curse the instrument

This is a harsh reality that is difficult to accept! Any amount of distress that we go through in life is the result of our past karma. Our karmic reactions manifest in various ways as mental distress, chronic disease, legal implications, etc. Others simply become instruments to give us what is meant for us.

Acceptance will reduce our pain drastically. When we accept that the distress is our doing, will we never blame anyone else for our pain. If we have indigestion, it is the result of eating something unhealthy. We do not blame our host for inviting us for a meal. Where is the question of resentment or revenge? Instead, knowing the science of karma, we will become sober and resolve to avoid any wrong actions in the future that could lead to similar pain in the future. Thus, our pain could actually become a catalyst for us to tread the path of righteousness.

Journaling and analysing

The more we carry pain in our hearts, the heavier the burden becomes. Write to feel lighter. Writing everything down, even about the wounds we think are long gone, is essential. We need to analyse by asking the following questions:

- How important is it for us to cling to this particular hurt?
- How is it helping me? Is it worth it?

- What do I want in my life? Do I want to free my heart from this emotion or should I hang on to it and stay in the shell of negative thinking, and torture myself?

Practice detachment

Once two travelling monks reached a riverbank where they met a young woman waiting to cross the river. Scared of the current, the young woman asked if one of the monks could carry her across. While one monk hesitated, the other quickly picked her up onto his shoulders, transported her across the water, and put her down on the other side of the river. She thanked him and then departed.

As the monks continued on their journey, the other monk became obsessed and preoccupied with his thoughts. Unable to hold his silence any longer, he spoke out. He said, 'Brother, our spiritual training teaches us to avoid any contact with women. But you picked the young woman up onto your shoulders and carried her across the river, thus breaking this most sacred rule.'

'Brother,' the second monk calmly replied, 'this happened many many miles back. It was I who carried the young woman and it was I who placed her down on the other side, over an hour ago. So why, brother, are you still carrying her?'

The function of intelligence is to discriminate and make the right decisions. Further, it is superior to the mind. Thus empowering intelligence, we must 'stop carrying the burden.' Do not sweat the small stuff. The more we think about something, the more we become attached to it and the more it weighs on us.

Patience

Time is the biggest healer. It is important to understand that if somebody has caused us pain, it will not be healed overnight no matter how much we try. Everything takes time to heal, especially emotional damage. Have patience. Time destroys everything, even our pain.

Pray

Do not ask God to remove the burden on your back but ask God to make your back strong. We have limited powers. We need to access the higher powers. There is somebody up there who is in complete control and waiting to reciprocate. We can pray, 'Dear God, please give me the strength I need to let go, the courage I need to move on, and the wisdom I need to learn from my mistakes.'

If we find it difficult to forgive someone, we simply need to bring Krishna's beautiful form into our mind and offer a humble prayer, 'Dear Lord Krishna, let me not act upon these emotions. Let me rise above them.'

Also, we can pray to have a grateful heart. 'Gratitude turns what we have into enough.' The Lord is situated in everyone's heart as Paramatma and He has declared in the Bhagavad Gita [5.29]

suhridam sarva-bhutanam
jnatva maam shantim ricchati

I am the greatest well-wisher of everyone

Anyone who understands this can easily achieve peace. So seek his grace. Grace can help the blind see and the lame cross mountains. Pray hard and you will never be let down.

Purify the heart

Unless the heart is fully purified, the pain will keep coming back. The greatest scripture Shrimad Bhagavatam, fourth canto talks of an interesting episode. Dhruva, a five-year-old boy, was the son of King Uttanapada. The king had two wives, Suruchi and Suniti. Suruchi, Dhruva's stepmother, was by nature very envious. She had a son named Uttama.

One day, Dhruva entered his father's court and saw his stepbrother sitting on his father's lap. Dhruva, being an innocent and loving child who loved his father, also wanted to do the same. His father, however, was more attached to his stepmother, Suruchi, and knew she would not like the co-wife's son to be given this special privilege. Thus he rejected Dhruva's affection and the child was hurt. Suruchi, to add fuel to the fire, insulted Dhruva saying he was not qualified to sit on the king's lap as he was not born from her womb. Dhruva, being a kshatriya, could not tolerate this and went away, hissing like a snake, to his mother in great anger and pain. She guided him to ultimately take shelter in the Supreme Lord because when no one can help, only He can. Dhruva now wanted revenge. He thought, 'I was not allowed to sit on the king's lap. So now I will show them by getting a position greater than ever occupied by anyone in this material world.' He left home for the forest immediately in search of God with an impossible desire in mind. When someone wants to approach God, He sends His representatives in our lives, a guru to guide us.

In Dhruva's case, the Lord sent Sage Narada to the middle of the forest. The sage first tested Dhruva on whether he was serious enough in his aspiration. When he was convinced, Sage Narada told him the process of devotional service. Along with controlling the mind and senses, he suggested chanting the Lord's names, meditating on His beautiful pastimes, and worshipping His deity form. And within six months, the Lord appeared before Dhruva. As soon as he saw the Lord before Him, all the impurities in his heart vanished and the anger against his stepmother and stepbrother was also gone. Dhruva was purified.

Similarly, we must allow ourselves the association of the Lord through the chanting of His names, hearing His glories and pastimes from the Bhagavad Gita, Shrimad Bhagavatam, and the Ramayana, worshipping His deity form and offering prayers, especially in the association of His devotees. Through this association, we shall purify our impure hearts and nourish our divine side and, thus, find it easier to let go of ill feelings.

We must view the pain and anger towards others as the impurity of our own hearts. Instead of blaming and criticizing others, focus on our own purification. Whatever happens to us is our destiny. How we respond to it is our choice. And the best response is to seek the shelter of the Lord to let go of the inauspicious situations. He is the abode of auspiciousness and when we bring Him into our life, He will take away all inauspiciousness and make our life supremely auspicious. In conclusion, let us resolve that the next time an unpleasant event happens, we will do our best to not take it personally. We will bring awareness to our thoughts and stop ourselves from creating a useless and unhelpful story. We will accept the situation as it is, and we will try to keep our reaction cool, calm and collected by drawing a mental barrier between us and the wrongdoer. We will react in a way that does not cause undue stress or unhappiness. Every time we face an unpalatable situation, mentally we shall offer a prayer to Lord Krishna, 'My dear Lord! Let me not act upon these negative emotions. Help me rise above. Help me let go instantly.'

IN A NUTSHELL

I was holding on to the past like an apple holds on to the branch of its tree.
At first, it felt like home, but when rain approached, it coerced me to be free.
Letting go of the branch, letting go of the past, I was merely at sea.
It was a torrid time of contrite, but that's just an essential part of life.
After nightfall daybreak follows, crosses are ladders that lead to heaven tomorrow.
The branch of the past is consigned to oblivion, and so is the sorrow.
It's time to let go, seeds of devotion now you need to sow.
The present is to grow, dissolving in tears is fabricating a foe.
Don't we all know that life's colossal mercies come from letting go?

CHAPTER 6

DEALING WITH TOXIC PEOPLE

Do you have a friend, a family member or a romantic partner who is really difficult to get along with? Do you feel degraded or manipulated around them? If so, it is possible that you have toxic people in your life. Toxic people require special care to navigate if you choose to continue with them. Maybe it is a manipulative family member or a coworker who cannot stop complaining about every little thing.

We have all had such people inject us with their poison.

Their damage lies in their subtlety and gaslighting. They can have us questioning our 'over-reactiveness', our 'oversensitivity', or our 'tendency to misinterpret'.

THINGS THEY DO

Toxic people can do anything to manipulate others to their advantage. These can be obvious as well as subtle. Knowing what to expect from them will help us navigate and even avoid their games. Here are some things they usually do.

They keep us guessing about which version of them we are getting

You'll find them being extremely respectful one day, and the next, they'll be giving you the silent treatment or acting as if you did something wrong. They will keep you in a loop of wondering what you've done to upset them. Rather than communicating effectively, they change their attitude towards you in a subtle way—you just know something isn't right. They might be prickly, sad, cold or cranky and when you ask them if everything is okay, the answer will likely be 'yes' or a 'hmm'—and yet they'll give you just enough to let you know something is wrong. They may express this with a heaving sigh, a raised eyebrow, a cold shoulder, or a passive–aggressive response. When this happens, you might find yourself making excuses for them or doing everything you can to make them happy.

They manipulate you

If you feel as though you are the only one contributing to the relationship, you are probably right. Toxic people often exhibit entitled behaviour. They take, and never give. They also have a way of doing something that hurts you, then gaslighting you into thinking they were doing it all for you. This usually happens in a workplace setup or a relationship with a power imbalance.

They will not own their feelings

Instead of taking accountability for how they feel, they will turn it around and call you 'unstable' or 'angry' or whatever they're feeling at the moment. This is called projection, which means they are projecting their feelings and thoughts onto you. For example, someone who is upset but will not take responsibility for it might accuse you of being upset with them. They may even say things like 'Are you okay with me?' or 'You've been in a bad mood all day', or a bit more pointed, 'Why are you angry at me?'

They will make you prove yourself to them

They'll constantly put you in a place where you have to choose between them and something else—and you will always feel obliged to choose them. Toxic people will wait until you have plans, and then they will insert themselves and guilt-trip you. Because they thrive on drama, they may even say things like 'If you really cared about me you would skip your exercise class and spend time with me.' This doesn't end with one incident. The minute you give into them, they ask for more, and it soon becomes a vicious cycle. The problem with this is that enough will never be enough. Few things are fatal—unless it is life or death, chances are it can wait.

They never apologize

Toxic people are chronic liars when the time arrives for them to apologize. Accept that there is no point arguing with them. They will twist the story in such a convincing manner that everyone, including themselves, will believe their nonsense instead of the truth.

They will be there for all your problems, but never to celebrate

Got good news? Your success is the toxic person's biggest fear. They come up with all sorts of reasons as to why what you've achieved isn't a big deal. Some example are: When you have a promotion, they say, 'The money is not that great for the amount of work you will be doing.' For a holiday at the beach, they comment, 'Well, it is going to be very hot. Are you sure you want to go?' It takes a while before an authentic person realizes that they don't need the toxic person's approval to go ahead in life.

They love leaving conversations hanging

They refuse to pick up their phone. Texts or emails will remain unanswered. By now, you find yourself feeling absolutely humiliated and even going through the conversation over and over in your head, wondering what exactly you said for them to start ignoring you in this way. Remember that these are all mind games. and anyone who loves you would never treat you so cruelly and let you go on feeling like rubbish without attempting to sort it out.

They will use non-toxic words with a toxic tone

While the message may seem harmless, its underlying tone has many implications. For instance, a simple inquiry such as 'What did you do today?' can hold multiple meanings based on the manner in which it is said. It could range from insinuating, 'I assume you did nothing, as usual,' to expressing dissatisfaction, 'I'm sure your day was better than mine. Mine was truly terrible. And you didn't even notice enough to ask.' When you question the tone, the response might be, 'All I did was ask what you did today,' which is technically true, but at the same time, not completely accurate.

They will bring unnecessary detail into the conversation

When you are trying to fix an issue with them, they will bring up things from the past, which were long forgotten and forgiven. Or so you thought. This could also result in a word salad, where they say a lot of things from old incidents and jumble it up. Before you know it, you find yourself feeling confused and begin to defend yourself or apologize. Again, this is manipulative behaviour. Somehow, it just always seems to end up about what you have done to them.

They will distract you

They will focus on the way you're saying something rather than what you're talking about. Yet again, you will find yourself defending your tone, your gestures, the words that you used or the expression on your face which you didn't even notice until they pointed it out—and so, the problem doesn't ever get resolved because you always seem to end up on another tangent.

They exaggerate

'You always ...' 'You never ...' are the words they use, and these words can come across very jarring. They feel like accusations hurled at you for no reason, and it isn't easy defending yourself. Understand that you will not win, and that is okay. You win when you realize it's not important winning against a toxic person, and that putting yourself first and protecting your peace is the most important bit.

They are judgemental

Toxic people can hold one thing you said or did against you, and keep bringing it up as if this was your personality in itself. Don't let them define you by your mistakes. You are more than that.

The detrimental effect

Toxic people defy logic in fascinating ways. Some are quite obviously unaware of the negative impact they have on the people around them, while others seem to get great satisfaction from creating issues and pushing people beyond their limits. Whatever their intentions may be, they always bring unnecessary drama and anxiety in the lives of people they surround themselves with.

It is important to not be stressed out from their behaviour because stress can have a long-lasting and detrimental effect on the brain. Even a few days of stress can affect our neurons in the hippocampus, a crucial region of the brain responsible for reasoning and memory. Weeks of stress can damage the dendrites, the tiny 'arms' that brain cells have, used for communication. This damage is reversible, but why must we put our brain through this constant state of hurting and healing? What is the need for it? Prolonged stress, lasting for months, can permanently damage our neurons, thus weakening the ability to think critically and remember information. Stress poses a significant threat to our overall well-being and affects our potential and performance in the long-term.

Therefore, toxic people who drive our brains into a stressed-out state should be avoided at all costs.

NATURE OF THE WORLD

When the Lord incarnates into this world, He is not subjected to any laws of karma. Regardless, he seems to go through some problems by way of which He tries to teach us that no matter who we are, as long as we are in this world, we have to go through trials and tribulations. It is the nature of the world we live in.

Most of the time when we talk about being troubled by others, it is our close ones. In Lord Rama's lila, who was the one who sent Him into exile? His stepmother. Who insulted Dhruva when he was just five years old? His stepmother. When Krishna was living in Dwarka, His own people charged Him with theft and murder and He had to prove that He was not involved in any kind of conspiracy.

Who subjected the little five-year-old devotee Prahlad to all kinds of problems? It was his father, the mighty demon Hiranyakashipu. The great scripture Shrimad Bhagavatam, seventh canto, gives a detailed account of what Prahalad had to go through at the hands of his father.

So when we complain that we are being troubled by our near and dear ones, that is because only the people close to us can hurt us. Only things we are attached to can bring pain. But this is not an unusual situation. This will continue to happen. If one person stops troubling us today, someone else will trouble us tomorrow. That is the nature of the world—dukhalayam, as says the Bhagavad Gita. We cannot complain about the waves when we are in the middle of the ocean.

One's greatness is not judged by the amount of wealth, power or beauty one has. Srila Prabhupada, the founder acharya of ISKCON, once said that the greatness of a person is judged by his ability to tolerate provoking situations.*

WHY DO THEY DO WHAT THEY DO?

There is a romantic saying, 'Someone somewhere is made for you.' It applies not just to romantic affairs but also to situations that involve toxic people. Even if everything is going well for us, even if there are thousands of people praising us, there will be at least one person or one situation that will make our life a living hell.

Why do these people behave in such a manner? This is because they are bound by their conditionings from the past, the present, and many past lives. They have misused their God-given free will and come to this point where hurting has become their second nature.

The Bhagavad Gita, the manual for human life, explains that toxic people's behaviour is because of the nature that they have been carrying from the past. This is why they never see an issue in their actions. It is very difficult for them to think otherwise due to the strong influence of past conditionings. In the Bhagavad Gita [7.14], Krishna says, '*daivi hy esha guna-*

* Quoted in Speakingtree.in, 'The Magic Talisman of Tolerance,' blog by Radhanath Swami.

mayi mama maya duratyaya'. It means, this divine energy of Mine (Maya Shakti) consisting of the three gunas (mode of goodness, passion and ignorance) creates these conditions and is extremely difficult to overcome as it is My energy.

It is almost impossible to change somebody's nature. 'Just like we may think that they are wrong, from their perspective we may be at fault. In the Mahabharata, when Lord Krishna goes to Duryodhana to remind him that he owes Pandavas their kingdom and tells him to return it, Duryodhana takes his time to answer. He contemplates for a long time and says after a long pause, 'I've thought about it. I thought about everything that has taken place since the time I was born but I do not think I have done anything wrong'. And so, Lord Krishna had to remind him of everything; how he tried to poison Bhima, how he tried to burn the Pandavas alive, how Draupadi was insulted, how the Pandavas were cheated of their kingdom, how they were exiled, and how they were insulted even while they were living in the forest. After hearing all this, Duryodhana still remains unmoved. He says, 'You know, Krishna, everybody's born with a particular swabhav (nature) and everybody's forced to act according to their swabhav. So I also acted according to my swabhav and I believe I am not responsible. It is ultimately the Vidhaata or Providence who has given me this swabhav. So you should blame him.'

Yes, we have that nature but it is not given to us by God. We have acquired it by our own free will by making certain choices in the past. The Lord is not responsible.

INSENSITIVE OR DESENSITIZED

We often use the word 'insensitive' to describe people. It is not that people are not sensitive, rather they have become desensitized. There is a difference. Insensitive means someone who does not care. Desensitized is when they do not even understand that what they are doing is wrong. Such people do not understand anything. It is just the nature that they have. For example, somebody picks up a musical instrument and starts playing. He thinks it is nice although he maybe tone-deaf. You cannot give feedback to such people because they will get offended. From their perspective, they are playing the instrument the best. How do you make such people understand? Some people love cleanliness whereas some people like to keep their surroundings messy. For them, it is natural. If we shout at them or tell them to keep things neat and tidy, they wonder why we keep troubling or shouting at them. We cannot make them think the way we do no matter how much we try. We cannot make them see sense.

THE SAFETY BUTTONS

Now that we know we are dealing with someone who is toxic, whether they are in our family, circle of friends or even workplace, it is time to act accordingly and protect our peace.

Being able to spot a toxic person's harmful behaviour is the first step to making sure you won't be affected. Although we cannot change them, we can change how we react to them. For this, we need to learn how to regulate our emotions.

The ability to manage our emotions and remain calm under pressure has a direct link to our efficiency. Authentic people are really good at managing their emotions in times that are stressful. No matter what, you will find them being calm and not reacting. Such people are also able to not fall for the dramatic tactics of toxic people. They possess excellent coping strategies that can keep toxic people scratching their heads.

How to deal with toxic people effectively? First, remember that you are always in control. That you don't have to step out of your personal power to negotiate with them.

The following tips can help.

Reject their version of reality

Often, you will find toxic people spinning a narrative that may seem truthful and believable, but remember they are good storytellers. They know how to play the victim or throw the blame on somebody else. Stay rooted in your own reality, and don't buy into their stories immediately until you can verify them. You can politely disagree with what they are saying, and it may hurt them, but hold onto your truth.

Once you have realized that they are toxic, why must you engage in their games? It is, after all, quite draining, and you absolutely don't have to fight with them or prove that you are right. Just walk away from their arguments and stop enabling them or giving them an opportunity to take up space.

Discuss their behaviour with them

Assess if the toxic person in your life is aware of their behaviour. Someone who gossips, manipulates others or creates dramatic situations might not realize how their behaviour affects you or anyone else. An open conversation may help them realize this behaviour is unacceptable. If you feel this person is acting from a place of ignorance and is willing to change if his/her toxicity is pointed out to them, then try having a conversation with them. To keep things neutral, try to stick to 'I statements', which feel less accusatory for the other person, and set boundaries that work for you.

For example:

'I feel uneasy when I hear unkind things about me.

'I value trust in friendship, but I cannot continue this friendship if you lie to me again.'

See where it takes you.

Empathy, empathy, empathy

Remember to always put yourself in the other person's shoes, even if it is not so easy. You don't need to be saving anybody or even agreeing with them, but always be kind. You can show them love from a distance, and you can deal with them politely without having to subscribe to their drama.

Draw boundaries

I know it is hard to say no to others, and a lot of us struggle with this. It is tough, especially when someone makes you feel guilty or behaves like the victim when you say no. But stay in your personal power, and understand that you are drawing that boundary for a reason. It is to protect yourself. When you begin removing yourself from toxic situations, you are actually engaging in self-love and will be in a better position to live a productive life.

Remind yourself that it is not your fault, even if they say it is

Toxicity is all about escaping accountability while making you feel like the bad guy. When being attacked by a toxic person verbally, remind yourself that this is on them, and not you. Let go of what they say, and never take it personally. They are behaving in a certain way because of their baggage, and it really has nothing to do with you. Forgive them and move on.

Don't be available

By making yourself less accessible, they lose their opportunity to target you. You stop being a vulnerable prey to them. This can be quite useful at work, because you can easily use work-related excuses to escape interactions that are toxic in nature.

Suggest help

Some toxic people are not malicious by intent, but rather because of their family problems or how they grew up or even incidents that hurt them in the past. To put it simply, they are hurt on the inside, and probably just need help. You can talk to them about finding a therapist that works for their issues, and you can even help them find the right one. Therapy is always good, and if a person is willing to go and work on their toxicity, then that is amazing.

Instead of focusing on the problems, think about solutions

It is better to move your attention to how you can handle the situation with the toxic person rather than constantly stewing over their bad behaviour. This way, you won't be stressed all the time, and you may even come up with a way to make things better for your own mental health.

TURN TO YOUR SUPPORT SYSTEM

When you have a toxic person in your life, especially someone you find hard to remove, it can get very suffocating and overwhelming. Remember to be compassionate towards your own self, and if you find yourself falling apart, always remember that you are allowed to seek help as well. You can reach out to the people who care about you and love you, and you can ask for their perspective and assistance. They might be able to look at your situation without bias, and even help you through it in a healthy way.

RISE ABOVE

Do not ask God to decrease the burden on your back. Ask God to make your back strong.' The more we focus on things that are within our control, the more we will be in peace. We cannot change the nature of this world or someone else's. The Shrimad Bhagavatam's perspective is that instead of trying to change the situations or other people, we should change our perspective. Changing ourselves does not mean that we suppress ourselves but that we transcend or rise above.

King Parikshit was supposed to die within seven days for no fault of his but how did he respond? He did not try to retaliate against the curse; he did not try to change the situation. He had the power to do so as he was a highly advanced devotee and extremely powerful. Even when he was in his mother's womb, the Lord personally protected him. The Lord appeared before him even before he was born. But he responded by absorbing his consciousness on the Supreme Lord, with whatever time he had left. He realized that there was something more important that he needed to focus on.

When we are faced with a negative situation, either we can complain or we can respond like King Parikshit. We can use every situation as an opportunity to come closer to God. Every time we do that, by the grace of the Lord, we rise above. Every time we give in, we become weak.

ACCEPT IT AS YOUR OWN STOCK

The Padma Purana says that the kind of people we interact with in this lifetime depends on our past. We have a karmic account to settle with them. The person is just an instrument to give us what we deserve. So learn to tolerate and do not retaliate. The more we retaliate, the more we implicate ourselves further in the karmic cycle. Acceptance reduces our pain by 70 per cent. Instead of criticizing or complaining and retaliating, we should accept it as our own karma. That is when we grow because the blame game stops and we are at peace.

THE ETERNAL NEED

Eventually, everything is meant to bring us to a point where we can turn to God and take His shelter. This is a material world and as long as we are on the material platform, the dualities of hate and love, honour and dishonour, and praise and criticism will keep troubling us. We have to transcend all this. And that can only happen by focusing our consciousness on God. So when we take time out every day to chant His name, remember Him, worship His deity form, pray to Him, we transcend. Then even if unpleasant situations manifest, we will not be affected by them at all.

This is the permanent solution that also helps us to deal with the karmic situation. The other techniques help us, but they will not help us beyond a point. They are immediate but temporary solutions. Ultimately whatever comes into our life, even a moment's distress, is a result of our own karma. The moment the Lord intervenes in our life, the moment we try to access that grace, He starts nullifying our karma. Karma ceases to act upon such people. And when karma is destroyed, the pain also stops.

In the Bhagavad Gita [14.26], Krishna explains

mam cha yo 'vyabhicharena
bhakti-yogena sevate
sa gunan samatityaitan
brahma-bhuyaya kalpate

(One who engages in full devotional service, unfailing in all circumstances, at once transcends the modes of material nature and thus comes to the level of Brahman.)

Lord Krishna says that anybody who engages in His unflinching devotional service can easily rise above his nature. So do not try to change a person because it is almost impossible. Only if they engage in unflinching devotional service can they rise above the 'gunas'. Instead, pray to Lord Krishna for them; 'My dear Lord, please engage this person in Your loving service. Please shower Your grace upon him.' Only by His grace and intervention can that person actually change.

In essence, we need to focus our consciousness on something higher when someone's toxicity bothers us. This way we grow and we do not have any negative feelings. And if our prayers are sincere, they will also change eventually.

Ultimately whatever is manifested externally is just a reflection of the consciousness that the person carries. But if the person is blessed by the Lord with divine consciousness, he will not act in a way that will bother anyone.

Some people cannot be pleased, some people will not be good for you, and many times that will have nothing to do with you. You can always say no to unnecessary craziness. Be confident and own your faults, your quirks and the things that make you shine. You do not need anyone's approval but remember, if someone is working hard to manipulate, it is probably because they need yours. You do not always have to give in but if you do, do not let the cost be too high.

IN A NUTSHELL

You spew negativity and blame it on me, manipulation in disguise of toxic glee.

Gaslighting me into believing I am crazy, presuming my memory is now hazy.

An apology from you is like getting blood of a stone, you are always talking in a strident tone.

No reciprocations, you are proud of your imprecations, your toxicity will not leave me alone.

In times like this, I approach the Lord, erudition the devotees accord.

You cannot change anyone, you can only change yourself, this cannot be ignored.

Opening the right doors in life will eliminate the toxic people rife.

Do not get drawn in, become thick skinned, let God take care of the toxic sins.

CHAPTER 7

OVERTHINKING: THE SILENT KILLER

Most of us have the habit of overthinking and more often than not, whatever we have thought has not turned out to be true. It has often been seen that 93 per cent of the things that we worry about never occur. In Hindi, there is a saying that the words chinta and chita have the difference of just one dot, otherwise, both are the same. Chinta means to worry, be anxious, overthink and stress. Chita means pyre. In the pyre, you burn only once, but chinta makes you burn every moment.

Overthinking makes us experience hell. It is explained in Shrimad Bhagavatam and Garuda Purana that when a person commits sinful activities, they are sent to hellish planets. As the soul is always eternal, we are given a subtle body in hell covering the soul known as 'yatna sharir' (body). Such a body is given to inflict yatna or misery, that is, punishment on the sinful souls. Having such a body makes one experience torture every moment and there are twenty-seven types of hellish planets.

On these hellish planets, the souls are in pain every moment. As they are already dead, they cannot die from the pain. And so, it is never-ending. Chinta is like that. Every moment we are dying but still, we are not dying.

There was a man who, one day, developed a phobia thinking people were after his life; he believed people wanted to kill him in the office. So, he stopped going to the office and stayed at home. Then he started thinking that his family was after his life. As a result, he started living inside his room with doors closed for everyone. The food plate would be passed to him from underneath the door. But then he thought his food was poisoned. So, he stopped eating and died a miserable death. All of this was because of overthinking, one of the symptoms of an uncontrolled mind.

Everything ultimately boils down to the condition of our mind. Even if there are a thousand causes of distress, we are safe as long as our mind is in good shape. On the other hand, even if there is plenty to be happy about, we will still be distressed if our mind is unhealthy. So, essentially, mind can create heaven out of hell and vice versa.

TYPES OF THINKING

Mind is so powerful that we can create, experience, enjoy and destroy things with thoughts alone. There are two types of thinking:

Thinking

It means to think as a preparation for action: 'What can I do? What action can I undertake if I have a problem?' You tend to think of the solution and, hence, this form of thinking is positive.

Overthinking

It means thinking as a substitute for action. When we do not take any action but simply keep thinking, it results in overthinking. A very common trait among all overthinkers is negativity as they tend to focus only on negative prospects.

Life is a journey from B to D, that is from birth to death, and between B and D comes C, that is, choice. And it is not always true that we will end up making the right choice every single time, and this holds true for everyone. What matters is that we should not be worried about making the wrong choices.

All humans are born with four defects: imperfect senses, tendency to fall under illusion, tendency to cheat and tendency to commit mistakes. Hence, no matter how much we try, we will not be perfect as we are born with these defects.

We might make mistakes, but that is all right. Instead of constantly obsessing over our mistakes, we must take action to work on ourselves. Worries, anxiety and overthinking do not solve any problems. But, in fact, working on a solution will solve the problem. Some people make things happen while some watch things happen, and some wonder what happened. The majority of people fall in the last category in this age of kali yuga. At times, things will not work out and when that happens, we need to figure out an alternative solution. Humans have a sharp intellect that can think of numerous solutions. Most importantly, the Lord is situated in everyone's heart as Paramatma, and if we tune into that frequency, the divine will guide us properly.

HOUDINI'S ILLUSION: PRISONER OF OUR MIND

There is only one prison that we all are living in and that is the prison of the mind. The famous magician Harry Houdini had given an open challenge that he could come out of any prison in the world within an hour and he had managed this feat on all occasions, leaving everyone in amazement each time. As a regular thing, once during a tour of Scotland, Houdini agreed to be locked up in the strongest jail cell available, boasting that he would escape from it. The magician was searched, his hands placed in steel handcuffs, and he was chained to a bench in the jail cell. The jailer shut the cell door and walked away, confident that Houdini would never escape. Left alone, Houdini quickly shed himself of the handcuffs and the chain binding him to the bench. Then he went to work on the cell door.

He tried every trick in the book to pick the lock on the jail house door. After an hour, he was dripping with sweat, apparently defeated. Totally discouraged, and near exhaustion, Houdini accidentally leaned against the door and it swung open easily, sending him tumbling into the corridor. The jailer had forgotten to lock the door. The door was never locked, but only in Houdini's mind.

Before we try to spend hours looking for a solution, we must make sure we have a legitimate problem. In other words, let us not overlook the obvious.

The phenomenon of Houdini's mind is depicted by the classic example of a bound elephant. A rope is tied to the leg of the elephant and there is a little stick in the ground to which the rope is fastened. The elephant is so huge that he can break cars and buses, but such a powerful animal is unable to break himself free. The reason is that the same rope and stick are used to tie baby elephants up to adulthood. As they are too small when they are babies to break free from the rope, they grow up being conditioned to think that the rope is stronger than they are, even though they grow more powerful by the day. As adults, they think the rope can still hold them, so they do not try to fight it. This is what our conditioning and thinking can do. The mind has the power to turn a perception into reality.

FEAR: THE SILENT KILLER

A man was once reading a newspaper in the park. Something bit him, and he thought he saw a rat running away while it actually was a snake. He remained calm as he assumed it was a rat. Then after some time, he got bitten again. He again looked and this time saw the snake. He was so frightened that he collapsed and died. Though he was bitten by the snake both times, the first time, he did not get affected because his mind was so strong that it did not let any fear overpower him. But the second time, fear took over.

In the absence of an enemy within, no external enemy can harm us. The mind is a powerful force, especially when it is uncontrolled. It can make us believe all negative prospects. So, what can we do? Thank the mind for its opinion and carry on and of course, focus on the positive prospects. It is the nature of the mind to constantly talk about how things could go wrong. Locked doors exist only within our mind, but the door to reality is wide open and all we need to do is walk through. Out of all the species of life, humans are the best and we have been given so much. We have been blessed with the ability to choose, experience an unlimited amount of bliss and make higher inquiries, but have still made our lives worse than animals. We have much better facilities to enjoy and make our life comfortable but with all this, what is the result? We are comfortably unhappy and stressed. Overthinking can kill not just physically but mentally too. It can destroy our relationships.

Overthinking makes us biased. Whatever fiction our mind has cooked from overthinking, we use it as a reference while dealing with people. This can cause many problems in our relationships.

If you are an overthinker, you will know exactly how it goes. A problem keeps popping up in your mind. For instance, a health worry or a dilemma at work and you just cannot stop dwelling on it, as you desperately try to find some meaning or solution. You keep on having the same thoughts but, unfortunately, you rarely arrive to a solution.

When we spend too much time analysing our problems and dilemmas, we often end up more at a loss than we were, to begin with. Moreover, persistent overthinking can result in a wide range of symptoms such as insomnia, trouble concentrating, and loss of energy, which, in turn, often leads to further worries regarding one's symptoms, thereby creating a vicious cycle of overthinking. In some cases, this eventually leads to chronic anxiety or depression.

However, there is good news. We do not have to live with excessive worry. It is an enduring myth that overthinking is an innate trait, like eye colour or crooked toes. Here are some ways to counteract the habit of overthinking:

Focus on the positive prospects

We will have to put in extra effort and endeavour to train our mind to focus on the positive prospects. Focus on what could go right rather than what could go wrong. People and situations do not make us anxious, but our mind does. Understand that the nature of an uncontrolled mind is to focus on only the negative prospects. Both right and wrong have an equal probability so why just focus only on the negative? Think positive. Thoughts can give us anxiety and thoughts can provide us relief too.

Have a plan b/prepare in anticipation

We cannot define our entire life by one mistake. We must learn to be kind to ourselves. To err is human. The point is to learn from those mistakes and move on. Always keep a plan b ready. And make yourself strong enough to deal with the worst-case scenario, as human beings are resilient by nature. You always have two choices: either keep complaining about the situation and play the victim or think of a solution to deal with the problem in the best possible way and become an inspiration.

Go deep

A powerful way to deal with negative thoughts is to neglect them and not take them seriously. The Bhagavad Gita [2.70] says:

apuryamanam achala-pratistham
samudram apah pravishanti yadvat
tadvat kama yam pravishanti sarve
sa santim apnoti na kama-kami

(A person who is not disturbed by the incessant flow of desires—that enter like rivers into the ocean which is ever being filled but is always still—can alone achieve peace, and not the man who strives to satisfy such desires.)

The mind of a spiritually advanced person is like the ocean. Thousands of desires enter his heart, just like thousands of rivers enter the ocean, but he is undisturbed due to his spiritual depth. A small puddle of water gets disturbed when it rains, and when there is drought, it dries up. On the other hand, the ocean is not perturbed by rains or droughts, it is always still, as it is very deep.

Hence, the Bhagavad Gita recommends we go deep into our spiritual life so that we do not get impacted by pride (when good things happen to us) or depression (when things are not favourable for us). We remain neutral irrespective of the situation. And for that, one needs to develop a divine consciousness.

Remember, we are not our mind or thoughts, so let them come and go. We can observe the thoughts, but need not act upon them. Intelligence is superior to the mind, hence we must use our intelligence to discriminate between wrong and right. And even stronger than intelligence is the soul, but we forget that and allow the mind to take control over us.

Intelligence gets sharpened by regular hearing and studying of scriptures that enables us to make the right decisions in life. It allows us to distinguish between which thoughts need to be ignored and the ones that need to be taken seriously.

Be grateful

Being grateful immediately uplifts our consciousness. Make a list of things you are grateful for: it can be related to your wealth, health or family. These are essentially the blessings in your life. Simply by penning things you are grateful for, you experience a boost in your mood. Radhanath Swami says that satisfaction lies in the hearts of those who are grateful. As the popular saying goes, you can choose to see the glass half empty or half full as it depends on the frequency you are tuned into.

Do whatever is within your control

Worrying will not get us anywhere. We need to act and do something to try to resolve the problem. Do whatever is within your control. Put in your best efforts and be detached from things that are not within your control. Efforts are within our control but not the results. Our growth and behaviour are within our control but not others' behaviour. So mentally draw a barrier as to what is within our control and what is not. Hence, cultivate a reasonable amount of detachment. This principle has been taught in the Bhagavad Gita [2.47]

karmany evadhikaras te
ma phalshsu kadachana
ma karma-phala-hetur bhur
ma te sango 'stv akarmani

(You have a right to perform your prescribed duty, but you are not entitled to the fruits of action. Never consider yourself the cause of the results of your activities, and never be attached to not doing your duty.)

Procrastinate

Whenever negative thoughts occupy your mind, procrastinate by saying 'I will think about them but later. Right now let me do something more important'. The mind is not used to being controlled. So initially when you apply the solution, it will howl and cry but when you learn to stop meeting the demands of the mind, the negative thoughts will eventually die out. Just the way the mind tricks us, we should also trick the mind. Anything auspicious, do it immediately. If anything is inauspicious, procrastinate it. Anything we procrastinate will never happen.

Take shelter of a spiritual mentor

On the battlefield of Kurukshetra, Arjuna became depressed as he slipped into the mode of overthinking. But he took shelter of his spiritual mentor, Lord Krishna. After gaining spiritual wisdom by listening to the Bhagavad Gita [18.73], Arjuna realized,

nashto mohah smritir labdha
tvat-prasadan mayachyuta
sthito 'smi gata-sandehah
karishye vachanaṁ tava

(Arjuna said, my dear Krishna, o infallible one, my illusion is now gone. I have regained my memory by Your mercy. I am now firm and free from doubt and prepared to act according to Your instructions.)

In other words, Arjuna said that he had gained complete clarity and now what he needed to do. Hence, it is important to take shelter knew of a spiritual master who can guide us based on the Bhagavad Gita. The Bhagavad Gita is the manual for life. When you buy a gadget from the market, it comes along with a manual that teaches us how to operate it along with the dos and don'ts. Similarly, the Bhagavad Gita teaches us what to do and what not to do. If one does come across such a spiritual mentor, one should be extremely grateful as rarely does a fortunate person come across a Guru and it is mentioned in Sri Chaitanya Charitamrita, Madhya 19 [Text 151]

brahmanda bhramite kona bhagyavan jiva
guru-krishna-prasade paya bhakti-lata-bija

(According to their karma, all living entities are wandering throughout the entire universe. Some of them are being elevated to the upper planetary systems, and some are going down into the lower planetary systems. Out of many millions of wandering living entities, one who is very fortunate gets an opportunity to associate with a bona fide spiritual master by the grace of Krishna. By the mercy of both Krishna and the spiritual master, such a person receives the seed of the creeper of devotional service.)

Coming across a bona fide guru or a representative of the supreme Lord Krishna marks the beginning of the end of all our worries. If we do not have him yet, we pray harder to the Lord to send one. Believe me, your life we be sorted forever.

Journaling

Pen your thoughts. When you write them down, you will realize how insignificant all your negative thoughts are and almost 50 per cent of your worry will be reduced. As the thoughts are now on paper, you can analyse them based on the wisdom of the Bhagavad Gita. You will gain better clarity and decide on what action needs to be taken to resolve the issues.

Pray

Whatever you lack or whatever situation you are going through, pray to Lord Krishna to help you. Brooding over things outside our control creates unnecessary resentment in life. His Holiness Radhanath Swami has written a beautiful prayer that we can say every day. 'Dear Lord! Wherever life takes me, please allow me to always keep *you* in my heart.' Another prayer we can say when it comes to overthinking is, 'Dear God, grant me the serenity to accept the things I cannot change, courage to change the things I can, and wisdom to know the difference.' We should say the above prayer regularly, as by doing so, we will be addressing our problems and anxieties. Surrender all your worries at the feet of Lord Krishna and His eternal Shakti, the most merciful Radharani, and you will witness all your anxieties and concerns vanish away. It is important to understand that surrender means to do what we can with what we have and leave the rest to the Lord.

Streamline sleeping pattern

The three hours of sleep between 10 p.m. and 1 a.m. is equivalent to six hours of sleep. This ensures that both body and mind are strong, ultimately resulting in powerful senses.

Hence, it is important to streamline the sleep cycle to have a powerful and controlled mind. In essence, it is all about our mind. Learn to make your mind your best friend and not your worst enemy. As Lord Krishna says in the Bhagavad Gita, one must elevate himself with the mind and not degrade, and this is possible only if the mind is willing to cooperate. This is only possible if we regularly chant and hear the mahamantra, the most powerful weapon to deal with the mind (mann)—Hare Krishna Hare Krishna, Krishna Krishna Hare Hare, Hare Rama Hare Rama, Rama Rama Hare Hare—and regularly study the scriptures such as the Bhagavad Gita and Shrimad Bhagavatam.

Do not get overpowered by your thoughts. It is we who make thoughts powerful. Focus on knowing what is right and doing what is right and leave the rest to the Lord.

IN A NUTSHELL

Caged in a cave, with no way back to the entrance, nor any escape.

In this cage called the mind, she is chained to her thoughts.

Focusing on the negative aspects of life is distraught.

There is always a right choice accountable for life's virtuous rejoice.

Yet, dwelling upon a wrong choice doesn't make it right.

We need to bear in mind God's name when in dire straits.

Overthinking is an internal battle that's not worth the fight.

An insignificant plight isn't cardinal enough to torture the mind.

Chant the Lord's name instead of overthinking to leave the fright behind.

CHAPTER 8

RESOLVING CONFLICTS

Conflict is a very normal part of the material world. We are all very different and it is natural for problems to arise when we interact with one another. Each one of us has our own needs, values and even habits, and therefore, misunderstandings can easily happen. We can get on one another's nerves and everyone need not agree to the same opinion. Conflict can also be healthy, because it makes people's boundaries clear. But at the same time, if it is unchecked, it can lead to relationships falling apart, morale dropping and even teams separating. Therefore, we must make sure that conflict is resolved.

Conflict occurs within ourselves as well. Our thoughts and cells are always in conflict. While all this is reasonable, it must also be noted that in this day and age, conflict has increased.

There are many disagreements over small matters, and this is a strong trait of the Kaliyuga.

Kaliyuga means 'kalah pradhan yuga' or a yuga predominated by conflict (kalah).

Conflict 101

- A conflict is not just another disagreement. In a conflict, things can get out of hand and there is a perceived threat.
- Conflicts continue to grow when they are swept under the rug. Had it been just another disagreement, people would let things go. But conflicts come with grudges and years of harbouring rage at the other person. There is no end to it until there is proper conversation regarding it.
- Response to conflict is biased. There is always going to be a wide spectrum of truths on the other end, and our truth as well. Nobody has the entire picture because the way we look at conflict is clouded by our upbringing, life experiences, culture, values and beliefs.
- Conflicts go hand-in-hand with your emotions. When a conflict arises, you may have noticed temperatures rising, fists shaking, people getting very personal about things. Conflicts can easily trigger grief, rage, jealousy and many other negative feelings.
- But we can grow with every conflict. Truly, it is a matter of perspective. We can either feel worse after a conflict and fester in our wounds, or we can come out of it with many lessons learned. Choose who you want to be in a conflict. The victim or the mature person, who has something good to take away from it?

Causes of a conflict

There are many reasons why conflicts occur. Like I mentioned, because we are all so different, our opinions or perspective of the world also differ. This means it is very easy to not agree with someone else's way of living, actions, choices or even ideas. For one person, it may seem like it is not a big deal, but to another person, it could be the end of the world. The important part is to address everyone's needs, respect them and try to put ourselves in their shoes.

A good example of how needs differ is this: a baby wants to explore the world. The baby does not think about anything except climbing on things and venturing out. But for a parent, the needs are completely opposite. The parent wants to ensure safety of the child. Together, they must come to an agreement so that both are happy and fulfilled.

For any relationship to succeed and thrive, there should be mutual respect of needs. Moreover, straightforward conversations should be had every time conflict arises so that the relationship can be protected. It is important to also take accountability and apologize when one is wrong.

How do you respond to conflict?

Many of us are afraid of conflict. When we think about conflict, we think about shouting or being angry at one another, but we must remember, not all conflicts are like that. Conflicts can be healthy and helpful as well, based on how we enter it. It doesn't have to be a traumatizing experience at all.

Many problems can be easily dealt with if we remain calm at the face of adversity. Instead of leaning on rage and other negative emotions, we can try to reign in how we feel. Respond, rather than react.

Healthy and Unhealthy Ways of Managing and Resolving Conflicts	
Unhealthy Way	**Healthy Way**
An inability to recognize and respond to the things that matter to the other person.	The capacity to empathize with the other person's viewpoint.
Explosive, angry, hurtful and resentful reactions.	Calm, non-defensive and respectful reactions.
The withdrawal of love results in rejection, isolation, shaming and fear of abandonment.	A readiness to forgive and forget, and to move past the conflict without holding resentments or anger.
An inability to compromise or see the other person's side.	The ability to seek compromise and avoid punishment.
Feeling fearful or avoiding conflict; expecting a bad outcome.	A belief that facing conflict head-on is the best thing for both sides.

Stress and emotions

In the face of conflict, you may find yourself battling some very strong emotions. But a healthy conflict has healthy results. Instead of bringing out stress, it can make us trust the other person more. In fact, when a conflict is resolved in a healthy manner, the relationship becomes stronger.

The first thing we need to realize is that it is important to be aware of our emotions. Emotions are necessary and should not be shut out. But at the same time, in a conflict, pay attention to the conversation that's being had. When there are no raised voices but mutual understanding and love, conflict can be dealt with well. Communication is key. Often we see that couples argue about things that feel trivial to the rest of the world. They may complain about how the other person doesn't keep their feet on the floor or that they eat too slow or something like that. Instead of addressing what is truly bothering them, they resort to pointing out simple character flaws. This is a sign that a deeper conflict was not resolved previously, and because of that, every small thing now appears magnified.

The one lesson to learn here is to deal with conflict immediately, before it blows up. If you have an issue with something someone said or did, bring it up kindly.

Don't bottle anything up.

THE WAY OUT

When conflict is mismanaged, it can cause great harm to a relationship, but when handled in a respectful, positive way, it provides an opportunity to strengthen the bond between two people. Whether we are experiencing a conflict at home, work or school, learning certain skills can help us resolve differences healthily and build stronger and more rewarding relationships. We can ensure that the process of managing and resolving a conflict is as positive as possible by sticking to the following guidelines.

Make conflict resolution the priority rather than winning or 'being right'

Our priority in life decides where we end up eventually. Resolving the issue and maintaining and strengthening the relationship, rather than 'winning' the argument, should always be your priority. Be respectful of the other person and their viewpoint. Generally, conflicts happen because both parties think they are right. Just because we are right does not mean that the other person is wrong. Everybody is an individual and from his or her point of view, they could also be right.

Be direct

Be open. Sometimes one person holds a grievance against the other but does not communicate. Instead of explaining why they are angry, they indirectly try to express displeasure through their actions such as by speaking harshly or by not speaking at all. The other person does not even know the cause of such actions and so does not have a chance to respond. Instead of indirectly expressing our displeasure, we can be direct and respectfully communicate. There could be a disagreement but mutual respect should always be there between two individuals. Do not be evasive, rather be mature and discuss. If we cannot do it, involve a third person who can communicate on our behalf in a dignified way.

Even if you are at the receiving end, apply the same principle. We can politely ask the person what action of ours is bothering them. If the person is not willing to come forward and discuss the reason for their sulky mood, we should not care. Why should we give our attention and energy to something that we do not even know? Unless a person is willing to come and express the reason for their disquiet, there is no solution expected out of the situation. Proper and direct communication is a must.

Discuss one problem at a time

If we hold on to grudges based on past conflicts, our ability to see the reality of the current situation will be impaired. Rather than looking at the past and assigning blame, we must focus on what we can do in the here and now to solve the problem. When there is a conflict, we drag the entire history into one problem. Avoid this at all costs. Discuss one problem at a time. Not every issue is connected and not everything needs to be connected. The circumstances that make a person behave in a particular way could be different at different times.

Think: could we be the cause?

There was a Japanese girl who had ill feelings towards her mother-in-law. The girl was unable to stand her bedridden mother-in-law and would always be angry with her. One day, she called her brother to express her frustration and how she hated her mother-in-law. The brother listened to his sister's rant quietly. Finally, he told her that he would be sending her a small sachet of poison that she should give her mother-in-law gradually over the next six months. After six months, the poison would kill her. But there was one condition; in these six months, the sister had to serve her mother-in-law with utmost care and love so that she would not suspect that anything was amiss. She had to be very attentive to the old lady's needs. The girl agreed, thinking it would be easy to fake love and care.

Six months passed and when the time came for the old lady to pass away, the girl called her brother again and broke down. She said, 'I am so miserable. Six months are getting over and now she will leave me. But now I do not want her to leave! I love her so much that I want her to stay forever. I cannot handle this!' The brother listened to her and laughed. He said, 'Actually, the poison was not in that sachet. The poison was within your heart, which I removed in the last six months by giving you a particular type of nectar. Even though you were faking your love for her at the start, you engaged in seva and that changed everything.' The girl was overjoyed to hear that the sachet did not have any poison and the poison from within her heart was gone.

So, sometimes we have to think like this as well, 'Maybe I am the one causing the conflict.' We need to introspect where we are wrong. We can ask someone we trust, and try to reconcile and rectify the situation.

Look for that 1 per cent right rather than that 99 per cent wrong

Whenever we are in a conflict with someone, our attention naturally goes to their mistakes and faults. We want to do things in one way; they want to do it in another way. However, focusing on faults makes the wall of hostility stronger.

To resolve the conflict, we need to conscientiously shift our focus to what is good and not what is bad. That shift brings us closer to a positive ground, where we can start talking with each other instead of talking past each other.

Often, conflicts escalate not just because of the issues, but also because of the emotions we bring to the issues. Starting with some positive emotions can offset extraneous negativities. The mind is such that whatever we focus on expands. Therefore, look for the good in the person. It will take some effort but if we want peace to end the conflict, we have to shift our focus from seeing faults to seeing one good thing that the person might have. And as soon as we do that, we will experience immense relief, almost immediately.

We have to be like a bumblebee and not like a fly. A fly sits on garbage even in a garden, whereas even in a pile of garbage, a bumblebee looks for nectar. Let us all be like the bumblebee. After all, at the end of the day, all we have is each other.

The great Vaishnava Acharya Srila Bhaktisiddhant Saraswati Thakur's method of dealing with a conflict was very simple. Whenever a resident or monk came to him with a complaint about another devotee, he would call both parties involved and make them sit in front of him and glorify each other. Soon they would forget each other's faults and the conflict would be over.

Never say never

Words can impact relationships. Never use the word 'never.' Avoid making statements such as 'You have never done this', 'You never listen to me', 'You never help me', 'You have never respected my family', among other things. This demeans the other person and puts them on the defensive, thereby making them talk along the same lines. Express! Express what is in your heart and express your present need. But avoid using the word 'never.' It creates a lot of negativity. Words have power and the more negative words we use, the more we create negativity around ourselves. Rather, we can begin by appreciating whatever good the other person has done for us in the past and gradually present the conflicting scenario. After all, everyone deserves the benefit of the doubt.

Pick your battles

Conflicts can be draining, so it is important to consider whether the issue is worth our time and energy. Maybe we do not want to surrender a parking space if we have been searching for one for fifteen minutes, but if there are dozens of empty spots, arguing over a single space is not worth the trouble. We do not have to fight every battle. It is always better to lose the battle of false ego.

Hanuman chose his battles carefully. A demoness called Simhika, the mother of the serpents, was sent by the devas to test Hanuman's intelligence and ability when he was flying to Lanka. She rose from the ocean, stopped his flight, and said, 'Nobody can go past this ocean without entering my mouth. I have received a boon from Lord Brahma and everybody has to become my food by entering my mouth.' Hanuman said, 'I am ready to become your meal for the day but I am on a mission now. Let me complete my mission after which I will come back and become your food.' She did not agree to this proposition. Hanuman used his intelligence and did not fight. He agreed to let her put him in her mouth. He expanded his size and in return, Simhika too expanded her mouth. Hanuman then became double that size and Simhika continued to expand her mouth until her lip was touching the sky. Then, Hanuman immediately shrunk in size, entered her mouth, and came back. He said, 'I entered your mouth, fulfilled your condition, and have respected the benediction that Lord Brahma has given you. So now I can leave'. Simhika was very happy and blessed him.

This is a classic battle of false ego. One is trying to outdo the other by becoming bigger and bigger. But Hanuman took a small position and evaded the conflict. Similarly, when there is a traffic jam, all the big vehicles are stuck but a cyclist or motorcyclist can easily manoeuvre and beat the jam. The smaller we are, the easier it is to sail through in this world. One does not lose anything by taking a humble position. Even if we are right in an argument, there is no big deal to say we are wrong. The other party will also realize this if we take a humble position. You end up avoiding unnecessary quarrels.

They also deserve a second chance

If a person's track record has been good, then they should be given a second chance. We should not pounce upon them on the very first mistake or fault they make. This is the mistake Bali committed with his brother Sugriva. A demon, Mayavi, attacked Kishkindha. Seeing both Sugriva and Bali together, Mayavi ran away and entered a cave. Bali went behind Mayavi and told Sugriva to guard the cave. For days there was no indication from within the cave whether Bali was alive. After one month of waiting, Sugriva heard a roar with blood and foam coming out of the cave. He did not know the reason and thought his brother was dead. He closed the cave assuming Mayavi to be alive, which would be dangerous for Kishkindha if he were to come out again. With a sad and heavy heart, Sugriva went back to Kishkindha and informed everyone of Bali's demise. He was then made the king.

But one fine day after killing Mayavi, Bali emerged from the cave. When Bali entered the court, Sugriva was so excited to see his elder brother that he came forward to embrace him. But seeing Sugriva sitting on the throne made Bali's anger increase a million times. He thought Sugriva had deliberately closed the entrance door of the cave. He pounced on him and eventually, Sugriva had to run away to save his life. Sugriva was the younger brother of Bali and from childhood, both had spent a lot of time together. As he was younger and based on his past record, Sugriva deserved a hearing. But Bali, without even asking for any clarification, beat him up. He had concluded that Sugriva was the culprit. The relationship remained strained till the deathbed reconciliation by Bali upon the intervention of Lord Rama.

In a big organization, an employee once became the reason for a few million dollars' loss to the company. Everybody spoke ill of him. One day, the chairman of the company asked to meet him. The employee was sure the objective of the meeting was to fire him. When he entered the chairman's office, he looked at the employee and said, 'I was going through the records and noticed that because of your efforts, the company has made so much profit in the past. Based on your past record, you can be forgiven for this particular mistake. So please get back to work.' On hearing this, the employee was so happy! In such a place where he is not judged for just one mistake, the employee would be willing to do anything for this company thereafter.

There are so many people in this world who like to create dissent between two people because of envy or jealousy. Always look for past records and do not give in to rumours. After all, the worst type of pain is when we are judged or misjudged, especially by our near and dear ones, whom we have given our lives for. We must avoid judgements as we would not like to be judged by others when we make a mistake.

Listen for what is felt as well as said

When we listen, we connect more deeply to our own needs and emotions and those of other people. Listening also strengthens, informs and makes it easier for others to hear us when it is our turn to speak. When they see that they are being heard, it resolves the issue to a great extent. Truly it works like magic.

Buy time instead of peace

Many times people get into a conflict but after some time, both or one of the parties involved try to make peace with the situation by saying, 'All right! I accept whatever you say. Let us end it here. It is not worth arguing.' They try to buy peace by agreeing to something that deep down they do not agree with. This results in anger, resentment and dissatisfaction with the individual involved and anger towards the person continues. This demonstrates a situation where our action is not in sync with what we truly feel and believe. It thereby creates unwanted hurt and unhappiness in relationships.

Hence, if we are habituated to saying 'yes' but there is a situation where we want to say 'no', we want to buy 'time' instead of buying 'peace'. Buying time means we do not have to immediately agree to something our heart differs with and instead seek time to prepare our script by outlining reasonable objectives that enable us to say 'no' at the right time. We can always seek time to think it over and then get back.

Be willing to forgive

Resolving conflict is impossible if we are unwilling or unable to forgive others. Resolution lies in releasing the urge to punish, which can serve only to deplete and drain our life.

Know when to let something go

If we cannot come to an agreement, agree to disagree. It takes two people to keep an argument going. If a conflict is going nowhere, we can choose to disengage and move on.

A family that prays together, stays together

We should make it a point, whether it is our family, society or an entire organization, to regularly come together for an activity where God is the Centrepoint. We quite often get together for dinners, parties and games. But when we congregate with a spiritual purpose in mind, a very powerful energy descends from that realm which dissolves our differences and binds us together. And the most powerful of all spiritual activities recommended for the present age of Kaliyuga is sankirtan: devotional chanting or singing of the Lord's holy names: 'Hare Krishna Hare Krishna, Krishna Krishna Hare Hare; Hare Rama Hare Rama, Rama Rama Hare Hare.' This simple process of sankirtan, when engaged in regularly, can miraculously make all issues disappear. We can even read or hear from scriptures such as Shrimad Bhagavatam, Bhagavad Gita, Ramayana and Mahabharata as a group or family. If we cannot do it on our own, we can invite devotees home to do it for us. Even if we can do it once a week, we will soon see the difference.

Shukadeva Gosvami says in the Shrimad Bhagavatam [12.3.51],

kaler dosha-nidhe rajann
asti hy eko mahan gunah
kirtanad eva krishnasya
mukta-sangah param vrajet

(My dear King, although Kaliyuga is an ocean of faults, there is still one good quality about this age: simply by chanting the Hare Krishna mahamantra, one can become free from material bondage and be promoted to the transcendental kingdom.)

Thus chanting the Lord's holy names can immediately counteract the ill effects of Kaliyuga. However, we need to have faith. Even though the solution is so simple, our complicated minds will make us try a thousand other things but sankirtan.

I want to recount a famous incident from the life of Srila Prabhupada. Srila Prabhupada's right-hand man, His Holiness Tamal Krishna Maharaj, a sanyasi, once came to him with a long list of problems to the temple he was staying in. Srila Prabhupada listened to everything and then said very casually, 'Do more kirtan.' This reply blew Tamal Krishna Maharaj away. He thought perhaps Srila Prabhupada had not paid attention to him. So he repeated all the problems again, to which Srila Prabhupada's reply was the same, 'Do more kirtan.' As Srila Prabhupada was his guru, Tamal Krishna Maharaj had no option but to follow his instruction. Tamal Krishna Maharaj started organizing the Hare Krishna mahamantra kirtan in the temple every Saturday for two hours. He then wrote to Srila Prabhupada, 'Miraculously, I do not know where all the problems disappeared. Everything vanished!' If one follows what the guru says, success will definitely come.

When there are problems, rather than fighting against them, try to get Lord Krishna in your life through His names, hearing His pastimes from the scriptures, service to His deity form, service to devotees and prayers, and see the wonderful magic that manifests. Lord Krishna is known as Hari (the one who steals) for two reasons: He steals our hearts through His unlimited sweetness and He steals away all kinds of negativity from our life. He is the supreme controller of all situations and when we allow Him to take control of our life, He does wonders.

Unless we spiritually clean our hearts of lust, envy, anger, greed, pride and illusion, there will be conflict within us and we will be tuned in to all the conflict around us. We must associate with people, activities and words that help us to tune in to those vibrations that will enlighten and elevate us rather than degrade us. We must surround ourselves with vibrations that bring us peace, happiness and love rather than passion, greed and ego.

Krishna means all attractive, reservoir of all pleasure, source of all love. When we chant the name of the Lord, what we are doing is tuning our consciousness to the spiritual channel that goes directly to the very essence of our heart and our soul, and connects us with the Supreme Lord. And through that influence, we are connected to all the energies, all the grace of the Lord, and that of the saintly people. When we tune ourselves to that vibration, we become influenced, moulded and cleansed, and rise above all conflicts.

IN A NUTSHELL

How does one ought to resolve conflicts, if their ego keeps depicting their pride?

The consistent intention to prove someone wrong, instead of resolving the fight.

The sentiment of feeding your ego by proclaiming to be right.

However, when there is a will, there is a way, your intentions determine whether you stray or stay.

Thoughts gradually manifest, so ponder about how to make amends today.

Kaliyuga is a sea of besetting sins, spirituality protects us from these material strings.

Conflicts are bound to happen, but being embraced by spirituality's support is the greatest win.

Do not let a negligible conflict turn the tables of life upside down, forgive from within, that is how a new day begins.

CHAPTER 9

OVERCOMING ENVY: THE UNFATHOMABLE VICE

Life is full of reminders of what we lack. There is always someone more successful, more talented, more attractive or more advanced in meeting milestones than we are. We encounter these people every day—in fact, they are often our friends, family members and colleagues. Sometimes these encounters can leave us with a bitter taste in our mouth and a green glow in our eyes.

WHAT IS ENVY?

It is a desire to be viewed as important. The 'I', 'me' or 'mine' is very prominent and originates from false ego. Often if we perceive someone to be a threat to our egoistic ideas, then there is negativity towards that person irrespective of who they are. It is a state of desiring something that someone else possesses. It is a vicious emotion that can crush self-esteem, inspire efforts to undermine others' successes or even cause people to lash out violently. It also just feels horrible.

There are six vices of the heart: lust that means selfishness, anger, greed, pride, illusion and envy. If one has envy within them, then the other vices are also present in them, which are lust, anger, greed, pride and illusion. It is important to understand the disease of envy is very difficult to deal with as it is destructive by nature and the last thing to leave our heart. The purpose of our existence is to be purified of these vices of the heart and regain our pure, spiritual nature.

THE DAMAGE IT DOES

An envious person hurts themselves more than they hurt others. The nature of envy is such that it makes us lose focus on the blessings that we possess. The constant focus of an envious person is what the other person is doing. Envious people carry negativity with them and it is so powerful that even if they are thinking negatively about us sitting three miles away, we may experience the discomfort. At times we may suddenly feel drained out for no reason and begin to experience negativity as we get impacted by their aura.

The definition of success for an envious person is not how much they have but how much the other person has lost. For instance, there was a person who was extremely envious of his neighbour. Once a genie appeared before him and asked what did he want? The genie, however, warned him that whatever he would ask for, his neighbour will receive the double of it. He did not pay heed to the condition and demanded a luxury car. The genie granted him his boon and a beautiful luxury car stood outside the man's house. He was extremely happy to see the car but his happiness vanished the moment he saw two luxury cars outside his neighbour's house. He went back to the genie and asked for the best bungalow. The genie again granted him his wish. When the man came out of his house for a stroll, he noticed that his neighbour had two lovely bungalows. He was again extremely disappointed. When the genie appeared again, the man said, 'Let me lose my one eye'. And when he went out of his house, he saw his neighbour running around blind. This made the man extremely happy. He then asked the genie if he could lose one arm and he saw his neighbour had lost both his arms. The man was immensely joyful. This is envy, a deep-rooted disease in which the envious person not only hurts others but hurts himself the most and derives the greatest pleasure in causing pain to others. '*Par dukh sukhi, par sukh dukhi*'. But for the one who is evolved his principle in life is, '*Par dukh dukhi, par sukh sukhi,*' that is, when seeing others in distress, he becomes distressed too and when seeing others happy, he becomes happy.

Envy prolongs our existence and misery in this world, and we end up implicating ourselves in the law of karma. A camel in the desert eats thorny bushes. As it chews the bushes, its tongue begins to bleed. But it enjoys the taste of its blood, not realizing it is hurting itself. Envy is exactly like this. The greatest self-destructive strategy is to act on our envy. Envious people are always on the lookout for spoiling the work of the people they are envious of and if that is not possible, they begin to spoil their name and reputation. It gives birth to back-biting and gossiping. Because they want to be seen as important but lack any inner substance, they try to feel important by making others feel or appear unimportant.

THE CLASSIC EXAMPLE

The classic example of what envy is all about is Duryodhana from Mahabharata. Being extremely envious of the Pandavas, he took away their right to rule the kingdom. He convinced his father, Dhritarashtra, to send away the Pandavas to Khandavprastha, a barren land, which the Pandavas transformed into a beautiful palace. After attending the Rajasuya yajna, performed by the Pandavas, where he saw all the kings of the different parts of the world had come to present the most valuable gifts to show their respect to King Yudhishthira and that they accepted his sovereignty, Duryodhana's envy grew exponentially. He even thought of committing suicide after witnessing the opulence of the Pandavas. He started plotting another conspiracy against the Pandavas and decided to invite them to a game of gambling. Dhritarashtra discouraged his son from scheming against the Pandavas and explained that the Pandavas had a small piece of land. He said the Pandavas had no intention of taking away the kingdom from Duryodhana. He asked Duryodhana to let the Pandavas live happily and enjoy the opulence that he possessed. Duryodhana replied, 'I do not understand what you are trying to convey. My mind is extremely turbulent and is only focused on how to usurp away the opulence of Yudhishthira.' An envious mind is focused on what others possess. Envy not only destroyed Duryodhana but his entire dynasty.

In Shrimad Bhagavatam, the fourth canto tells the episode of Lord Shiva and Goddess Sati. She was the daughter of Daksha Prajapati, who was one of the sons of Lord Brahma. He was handsome and very powerful. He had given the free will to his daughters to choose their desired spouses. Sati had chosen Lord Shiva. While Lord Shiva provided all the opulence to his devotees, he lived a simple life. For ornaments he wore snakes, lived in a crematorium, had ashes smeared all over his body, wore deer skin and had knotted hair. As Daksha Prajapati belonged to an aristocratic family, he was not happy with Sati's choice of spouse. He once organized a yajna where he invited rulers from all over the universe. Though he did not like Lord Shiva, he was forced to invite him as he was his son-in-law. Daksha Prajapati forgot that Lord Shiva was not only his son-in-law but also one of the most powerful rulers of the universe. He is the incarnation of Lord Sankarshan, an expansion of Lord Krishna. His aristocratic birth and status made Daksha Prajapati immerse himself in his false ego and pride.

When Daksha Prajapati entered the yajna arena, everyone stood up in awe of his effulgence except Lord Brahma and Lord Shiva. Daksha Prajapati did not mind that Lord Brahma had remained seated as he was his father and guru. But he was extremely angry at Lord Shiva. Furious he said, 'Oh rulers of the universe! Whatever I am saying, please note that I am not saying it out of envy...' and began cursing Lord Shiva in such a way that many other rulers could not withstand it and left the place. Even Lord Brahma left, but some supporters of Daksha Prajapati agreed with him. The scriptures state that if someone is insulting a devotee either defend him or leave the place or else you will also get implicated in the same offence. Harming a great soul is considered the biggest offence in the scriptures and is extremely dangerous for a person doing so as the Lord takes such offences very seriously.

Lord Shiva had not stood when Daksha Prajapati entered the arena as he was in samadhi—a state of deep meditation. He remained unaffected and left after a while. After some time, Daksha Prajapati organized another yajna and invited everyone but Lord Shiva and Goddess Sati. However, Sati had a strong desire to attend the yajna and meet her family. Lord Shiva warned her against attending the yajna as she would not be able to withstand him being blasphemed. Sati was extremely upset and angry with Lord Shiva and decided to attend the yajna against his wishes. When she entered the arena, Daksha Prajapati neither spoke to her nor welcomed her. She was very angry to see that there was a designated place for everyone in the yajna except for Lord Shiva. She shouted at her father and said, 'The worst thing I have got from you is this body and I shall renounce it today itself.' And she invoked the fire element of her body and reduced herself to ashes. When this news reached Lord Shiva, in extreme anger, he sent his ganas, led by Virabhadra, who cut off Daksha Prajapati's head. Later Daksha Prajapati sought forgiveness and Lord Shiva gave him the head of a goat as his pride was smashed. This is the extent to which envy can destroy us. The sooner we realize we have envy within us the better, and we should immediately try to cure the disease.

PRACTICAL TIPS TO HANDLE ENVY

Assume that they need it

No situation, nor a person, has the power to make us feel envious unless we have it in our heart. So, the problem is with us, and we need to learn how to trick the mind as everything gets manifested through it. When you see something, the mind starts analysing it and you get paralysed. It is paralysis by analysis. Instead of becoming envious, tell yourself that the other person requires more than you as you do not know what the other person is going through in their life. This way you will be able to trick the mind. So when you see someone getting something better, think that they need it.

Maybe they deserve it

Understand, life is a multi-innings game. The other person must have done something nice in their previous birth because of which they have become what they are today. Instead of getting depressed that someone has more than us, we should get encouraged and inspired by the system within the universe. Tell yourself that by doing good today, even I can have such things in the future. By adopting such a mindset, we will contribute to our growth. Otherwise, envy has the potential to cripple our growth.

Identify your need

Envy tends to make us lose focus of our blessings and things that we already possess. Learn to focus on your need and simplify your thoughts. When you do so, you will realize that what you need, you already have in your life. Keep in mind the bigger picture that human life is given to us for self-realization and God-realization.

When envious thoughts trouble you, stabilize yourself and focus on, 'What is it that I need? And what difference will it make if the other person has more than me?' Moreover, you need to fulfil your spiritual needs and not just your material desires. In fact, spiritual needs should take precedence over material requirements as we are spiritual beings.

Cultivate the quality of satisfaction

Learn to be happy with whatever you have. Accept it as the outcome of your past karma and focus on your blessings. By doing so, your blessings will expand as whatever the mind focuses upon, it expands.

Do not compare yourself with others

Everyone is an individual soul and everyone has their weaknesses, strengths and struggles. Some people may possess things you do not have and vice versa. Comparing, criticizing and complaining are the cancers of the mind. Hence, do not compare, as things will not change. Focus on the gifts given by God to you and let others focus on their gifts. Every individual has their journey in life; we come into this world alone and have to go back alone.

When we compare ourselves with others, it means we are trying to find fault with the Lord's creation. Remember, the situation the Lord has put us into is perfect for us. Everything we witness in our lives is orchestrated by God and His energies for our growth. You do not need to pull someone down in life to grow. We do not have to depend on another's failure for our success. Where attention goes, the energy flows. So, focus your attention on your growth and not on the downfall of others.

Philosophical analysis

Focus on the bigger picture: self-realization and God-realization. Ask the right questions: Who are we? Why are we here? We are spiritual beings and souls living in the material body. And when this body becomes unfit for living, we move into another body. Hence, if we are the souls, then no amount of material arrangement can satisfy us. If we do not belong here, why do we hanker after things on a material platform? Our goal is to wind up our obligations in the material world and not compound them. Our goal in human life is to go back to the spiritual world after we leave this body and to achieve that, we must become attached to what is spiritual. We are just passengers, here to spend some limited time. Let us not worry about what others have or are doing. We should focus on our journey to our destination.

Engage in the devotional service of the Lord

Only when we engage in the Lord's devotional service and practices, do we find inner fulfilment and contentment. For instance, if you are hungry, you will search for food. On the other hand, if you are not hungry, then you will not even care what others are eating as you are completely satisfied. We are envious of somebody as we lack that fulfilment and assume if we possess the thing the other person owns, we will be satisfied and happy. The need for contentment and fulfilment cannot be satisfied through material possessions or arrangements since we are not matter, but spirit souls. Only when we connect to our original spiritual nature, we will feel truly satisfied. Instead of filling ourselves with envious thoughts, we should try to fill our hearts with Lord Krishna, our source and whose parts and parcels we are.

Devotees are so content in the Lord's devotional service, that is hearing about the Lord and chanting His holy names, that they are not bothered or impressed even with Lord Brahma's position, the topmost position in the material world.

Therefore, no amount of material attainments can satisfy us but by chanting the holy names of Krishna in the form of the Hare Krishna mahamantra, 'Hare Krishna Hare Krishna, Krishna Krishna Hare Hare; Hare Rama Hare Rama, Rama Rama Hare Hare,' hearing from Shrimad Bhagavatam, reading the Bhagavad Gita and worshiping Lord Krishna's deity form regularly. You will witness the disease of envy gradually diminishing.

As envy is a disease of the heart, it needs to get purified. Madhya-lila, Sri Chaitanya Charitamrita [22:107] says,

nitya-siddha dayaa-prema 'sadhya' kabhu naya
shravanadi-shuddha-chitte karaye daya

(Pure love for Krishna is eternally established in the hearts of the living entities. It is not something to be gained from another source. When the heart is purified by hearing and chanting, this love naturally awakens.)

By intensifying Lord Krishna's consciousness, that is, by hearing and chanting the Lord's name, our hearts get purified. So the ball is in our court to cure the disease of envy within us. When someone receives something better and more than us and if we feel happy about it, we should understand this permanent solution is working and we are getting freed from envy. When we take pleasure and celebrate others' success, we understand that we are evolving and becoming pure, free from envy.

Envy takes lifetimes to cultivate and it will not go overnight. We must have patience. However, we must try and work towards purification and simultaneously pray for Lord Krishna's grace. Our efforts are limited but His grace can change things in a moment. When He is pleased with our efforts, He will bestow

His causeless mercy that will create magic in our lives. Never underestimate the power of prayers. Whatever we pray for, Lord Krishna will grant. Show by your efforts that you wish to be free from this monster of envy and He will supply whatever we lack. Do your best and leave the rest to Him.

IN A NUTSHELL

Ever seen a man starve right after devouring a filling meal?
Guess it is human tendency to want what we do not need.
Desire, jealousy, envy, we cannot bear the thought of our plate being empty.
Ever seen a dissatisfied man who has the world at his feet?
Guess it is human tendency to befall greed for self-conceit.
Envy sails under the false colours of self-destruction, us humans keep turning away from our resurrection.
Ever seen the eyes of a man stuck to another's plate?
Guess it is human tendency to yearn another's fate.
Abundant mercy on your plate, yet your neighbour holds your attention as bait.
In the spiritual world, every meal is a blessing, even the smallest gift is worth caressing.
The Lord forbids selfishness, pay no heed to greed, when the act of sharing is progressing.
Snap out of the material world, anticipate your needs, God is giving you what you deserve, take it with glee.

CHAPTER 10

OVERCOMING ANGER: THE GATEWAY TO HELL

Speak when you are angry and you will make the worst speech of your life.

—Laurence J. Peter*

We all know what anger is, and we have all felt it: whether as a fleeting annoyance or as full-fledged rage. Anger is a completely normal, usually healthy, human emotion. But when it gets out of control and turns destructive, it can lead to problems—problems at work, in our relationships and in the overall quality of our life.

Anger can make us feel as though we are at the mercy of an unpredictable and powerful emotion. Lord Krishna describes anger as the gateway to hell in the Bhagavad Gita

* *Peter's Quotations: Ideas for Our Time* (Collins Reference, 1993).

[16.21]. However, it is not always bad if channelized properly. When Arjuna had to fight the Kauravas in the great war at Kurukshetra, he was not doing it with a smile. He was angry and his anger was justified as he was fighting to protect dharma, for the benefit of the people at large. Similarly, in the Ramayana, when Laxman disfigured Surpanakha's nose, she went to her brothers, Khara and Dushna in the Dandaka forest (present in Nasik), crying and moaning in pain. She instigated Khara and he sent fourteen of his most powerful rakshasas who were easily killed by Lord Rama. After that, fourteen thousand more were sent. It is mentioned that when Lord Rama saw that army of demons coming, he summoned His all-powerful anger.

But anger becomes the most destructive or negative emotion when it is expressed as an emotional outburst and meant to harm others. It destroys us and also destroys all those around us. 'Anger is nothing but one letter short of 'danger'. It arises due to unfulfilled expectations or desires. We want things to go our way. When they do not, we get angry.

Thus, it is a common response to frustrating or threatening experiences. It can also be a secondary response to sadness, loneliness or fear. In some cases, the emotion may seem to arise from nowhere. From the Bhagavad Gita's perspective [2.62]

dhyayato vishayan pumsah
sangas teshupajayate
sangat sanjayate kamah
kamat krodho 'bhijayate

(While contemplating the objects of the senses, a person develops an attachment for them, and from such attachment lust [obsessive desire] develops, and from lust anger arises.)

In these two verses, Krishna explains how anger actually arises and how it ultimately makes a person fall and leads to the degradation of the soul.

As in the Bhagavad Gita [2.63]:

krodhad bhavati sammohah
sammohat smriti-vibhramah
smriti-bhramshad buddhi-nasho
buddhi-nashat pranashyati

(From anger, complete delusion arises, and from delusion bewilderment of memory. When memory is bewildered, intelligence is lost, and when intelligence is lost, one falls again into the material pool.)

We see something and we keep thinking about it. This makes us attached to that particular thing which gives rise to a desire to obtain that object. If we get it, it gives rise to greed. If we do not, we get angry. From anger comes complete delusion and bewilderment of memory. We forget everything: what is right and what is wrong. When memory is bewildered, intelligence is lost. The function of intelligence is to discriminate between right and wrong and that power is gone. When intelligence is lost, one ends up committing acts that lead to a person's downfall. In essence, anger clouds our intelligence, as a result of which we end up doing things we are not supposed to do.

THE DISASTROUS EFFECTS OF ANGER

Loss of pious credits

When a person gets angry, he loses his pious credits. Whatever good the person has done and the credits he has earned are lost. In the Ramayana, there is a wonderful story about a quarrel between the great Sage Vishwamitra and Sage Vashishth. Vishwamitra was a king. Once, King Vishwamitra went on a hunting excursion with his army. Feeling hungry and thirsty, they reached Sage Vashishth's hermitage who took good care of all of them. King Vishwamitra noticed that Sage Vashishth had nothing except a small cottage and wondered how he managed to feed thousands of soldiers and horses and elephants as well. On enquiring, he came to know that Sage Vashishth had a Kamdhenu or a desire-fulfilling cow. King Vishwamitra was astonished to know that a sage possessed such a divine being while he, being a king, did not have anything like it. After finishing his meal, the king met the sage again before leaving for his palace. He tried to convince Sage Vashishth to give him the Kamdhenu in exchange of hundred thousand cows but failed. Listening to this, the king upped his bid and said that he would give fourteen thousand elephants, eleven thousand thoroughbred horses loaded with gold, eight hundred chariots made of gold (each harnessed with four white horses), ten million cows of all colours, and any amount of gold that the sage would wish for. But yet again, King Vishwamitra's offers met with Vashishth's firm refusal. Sage Vashishth said that there was nothing that the king could possibly offer him which would make him give up Kamdhenu. He also emphasized the fact that Kamdhenu was not a mere asset but a member of his ashrama. Enraged by this, the king ordered his soldiers to capture the cow and bring it with them anyways. The Kamdhenu tossed the soldiers and went to Sage Vashishth. She begged him to save her from this malicious army of the arrogant king. In a helpless voice, Sage Vashishth said that he did not have an army to fight against the king.

To that Kamdhenu said that she would provide the sage with an army of his wishes. Instantly, Kamdhenu manifested many warriors from her body and defeated Vishwamitra's army.

Seeing this destruction, the sons of Vishwamitra rushed towards Vashishth. The sage uttered only one word and all of them were reduced to ashes. Devastated, King Vishwamitra marched back to his capital city. He then crowned his only remaining son and took off to the forest to do penance. After years of austerity and penance, he was able to please Lord Shiva who asked him to wish for a boon. Vengeful Vishwamitra asked for knowledge of all weapons and warfare so that he could use it against Sage Vashishth. Lord Shiva granted him the boon.

Vishwamitra was now dead set to take revenge against Sage Vashishth for the death of his sons. He again went to Sage Vashishth's hermitage and set ablaze the abode of several hermits, including Vashishth's, with his newfound powers. It was utter chaos as everyone started running helter-skelter to save their lives. Sage Vashishth came out and challenged Vishwamitra. Vishwamitra threw divine weapons to kill Vashishth but to his surprise, Vashishth was able to absorb everything within his staff. Even when Vishwamitra threw the Brahmastra, it got absorbed in Vashishth's staff. Everything that Vishwamitra had was rendered useless against the spiritual powers of Sage Vashishth. In the end, he fled and went back to his kingdom.

King Vishwamitra realized that the brahma-tejas or the power of a brahman is greater than his kshatriya (warrior) power and thus he resolved to perform penance to please Lord Brahma and become a 'Brahma Rishi'. He underwent severe austerities for a long time. Feeling insecure that Vishwamitra was performing austerities to take over his heavens, Indra, the king of heavens, sent an apsara (a heavenly damsel) named Menaka to spoil Vishwamitra's meditation. When Vishwamitra heard the tinkling of her anklets, his meditation broke. He fell in love with her and even had a family with her. He named their daughter Shakuntala. It was then that he realized, he had wasted the results of all his penance. He immediately started performing severe austerities. His years of penance and fame spread all over the universe. Indra again sent another apsara to disturb Vishwamitra's meditation, but this time he was determined not to fall into the same trap. As soon as the apsara came, he opened his eyes. Two flames shot from his eyes which burnt her to ashes. The apsara was gone but immediately the powers Vishwamitra had gained till then were destroyed. He was remorseful that he had lost the results of all his penance because of his anger. Thus anger not only destroys us at a physical level but also at a spiritual one. It wrecks our intelligence and piety. In no way is anger beneficial unless it is meant for the benefit of someone, that is, to protect the innocent or dharma.

Later, when Sage Vishwamitra came to Ayodhya to seek King Dasharatha's permission to take Rama and Laxman to his hermitage, the king hesitated. He was not aware of the divinity of his two children, especially the firstborn. Vishwamitra had by then become a brahmarishi and was completely purified at heart. He had no enmity towards Sage Vashishth. It was Sage Vashishth who convinced the king to send his sons with Sage Vishwamitra. Sage Vashishth told King Dasharatha, 'Understand that Vishwamitra wants your son Rama to increase His fame. Vishwamitra too is capable of destroying the demons but he does not want to do it because it will destroy all the pious credits he has gained. The demons are attacking him and he wants to avoid losing his power. More than that he wants to increase your son's fame.' These words convinced King Dasharatha to send his sons with Sage Vishwamitra.

Heart's distance

There was once a sage travelling with his disciples. On reaching the banks of the holy Ganga, he saw some people arguing with each other. The sage smiled and asked his disciples, 'Why do we shout when we are angry? Look at those people. Even though sitting next to each other, they are shouting at each other.' The disciples gave different answers but none pleased the sage. Finally, the saint explained, 'When two people are angry at each other, their hearts distance a lot. To cover that distance they must shout to be able to hear each other. The angrier they are, the stronger they will have to shout to cover that great distance. What happens when two people fall in love? They do not shout at each other but talk softly. This is because their hearts are very close. The distance between them is either non-existent or very small.' The saint continued, 'When they love each other even more, what happens? They do not speak, only whisper. Finally, they even need not whisper, but look at each other and that is all. This is how close two people are when they love each other.'

He looked at his disciples and said, 'So when you argue, do not let your hearts get distant. Do not say words that distance you from others or else there will come a day when the distance is so great that you will not find the path to return.'

The irreversible damage

There once was a little boy who had a very bad temper. His father handed him a bag of nails and said that every time the boy lost his temper, he had to hammer a nail into the fence. On the first day, the boy hammered thirty-seven nails into the fence. The boy gradually began to control his temper over the next few weeks, and the number of nails he hammered into the fence slowly decreased. He discovered it was easier to control his temper than to hammer the nails into the fence.

Finally, the day came when the boy did not lose his temper at all. He told his father the news. The father suggested that the boy should now pull out a nail every day he kept his temper under control.

The days passed and the young boy was finally able to tell his father that all the nails had been pulled out from the fence. The father took his son by the hand and led him to the fence. 'You have done well, my son, but look at the holes in the fence. The fence will never be the same. When you say things in anger, they leave a scar just like this one. You can put a knife in a man and draw it out. It would not matter how many times you say I am sorry, the wound will still be there.'

The wounds caused by a knife can still be healed but the ones caused by words are impossible to heal. Anger does not solve anything. It builds nothing but can destroy everything. Anger is a punishment we give to ourselves for somebody else's mistake.

Hope

Although controlling anger is a challenge and we all are aware of the damage it can do and the guilt it can cause thereafter, there is always hope. There is always something we can do to minimize the damage. We are not programmed robots and we can change. We may be born with a particular nature but that cannot be the excuse to lash out at someone. We can and must try to change if we realize our faults. Here are a few strategies that can help us deal with uncontrolled anger issues.

Have a reality check

We are not the centre of the universe. We are not so important. We are insignificant. The most important thing we need to remind ourselves, again and again, is to have a reality check; why does anger arise? Because we want things to go our way, we want people to behave the way we expect, we want to be in control. The reality, however, is different. We are not in control. We may have some control but not complete control. There will be moments of success and moments of failure. This is how life is. Life is unfair, but we can always make the best of it. Introspect, always stay in touch with your inner self and stay rooted to reality.

Cultivate forgiveness

In the Mahabharata, the great Bhishma, lying on a bed of arrows, explains to Yudhishthira that to control anger, one must cultivate the most divine quality of forgiveness. It is impossible to sustain peace or any relationship without cultivating this quality. There is no way around it. We have to work on this. Unfortunately, we do not make an effort to cultivate this divine quality in ourselves but we expect it in everyone else.

We need to forgive minor mistakes. Sometimes even some of the bigger mistakes have to be forgiven because to err is human and to forgive is divine. Everyone makes mistakes, everyone has faults and we are no exception. Stop looking for perfection. Sometimes, people will do the right thing and at other times, they will make mistakes. Whether it is our partner, children or colleagues, they will all make mistakes. For our peace of mind, we must learn to forgive. Rather than shouting at somebody, forgiveness, more than anything else, will make that person more loyal to us.

So when we are angry, rather than forgiving, we are blaming the opposite person and finding faults. And no human being likes to hear their faults. Apart from inciting negative emotions and the worst in them, it only makes them defensive and insecure. Forgiveness brings out the best in the person.

Sometimes we might have to be vocal to correct somebody, but it should be done with compassion to help the person grow and correct their mistakes. When we do it as an emotional outburst, we bring out the worst in the person. As we want to be judged by our intentions and not actions and would like to be forgiven when we make mistakes, similarly we have to learn to judge people by their intentions rather than actions. Forgiveness is divine and we forgive for our benefit.

Keep good association

We become what we associate with. The kind of people we associate with will decide which type of nature is nourished in us. Thus we should associate with those people who can bring out the best and not the worst in us. According to the Bhagavad Gita [Chapter 16], we have two types of nature: the divine and the demonic. Associate with divine people. Take time out to be around saintly and divine people who can nourish our divine nature.

If our association is with people who have anger, greed, pride, illusion, envy, and all kinds of bad habits, then that is what we become. As they say, 'Tell me who you associate with, and I will tell you who you are.' It is that simple. When we say association, it is not limited to association with people. It also means association with the kinds of things we watch, the kind of things we hear and the kind of things we read. We must read scriptures and hear from the right people because, it is not the words that cause the transformation of energy but the consciousness behind those words. So we have to avoid the association of catalysts, which can incite that base propensity or the anger within us.

For example, it was found that the violence in media the young minds consume has an impact on them. No doubt, they imbibe it very quickly and begin to imitate it as well.

Virtually since the dawn of television, parents, teachers, legislators and mental health professionals have wanted to understand the impact of television programmes, particularly on children. Of special concern has been the portrayal of violence, particularly given psychologist Albert Bandura's work in the 1970s on social learning and the tendency of children to imitate what they see.

As a result of fifteen years of 'consistently disturbing' findings about the violent content of children's programmes, the Surgeon General's Scientific Advisory Committee on Television and Social Behavior was formed in 1969 to assess the impact of violence on the attitudes, values and behaviour of viewers. The resulting report and a follow-up report in 1982 by the National Institute of Mental Health identified these major effects of seeing violence on television:

- Children may become less sensitive to the pain and suffering of others.
- Children may be more fearful of the world around them.
- Children may be more likely to behave in aggressive or harmful ways toward others.
- Research by psychologists L. Rowell Huesmann, Leonard Eron, and others starting in the 1980s found that children who watched many hours of violence on television when they were in elementary school tended to show higher levels of aggressive behaviour when they became teenagers. By observing these participants into adulthood, Huesmann and Eron found that the ones who'd watched a lot of TV violence when they were eight years old were more likely to be arrested and prosecuted for criminal acts as adults.

A survey conducted at a primary school in Belica, Croatia showed that 91 per cent of the parents believed that violence on television will make their children act violently after watching it.

So keep good association, be careful of what we give our energy and time to and say no to temptation, especially that of anger. Learn to say no. The power to say no will come from the association that we keep.

Procrastination

If you sense that you are getting angry at somebody, procrastinate. When you delay, you do not end up getting angry at all. I have tried this too. Sometimes if I am getting frustrated with something, I try to delay the outburst a little bit. Then after maybe after five minutes, the feeling of frustration completely disappears from my mind. Anger is like that; it is momentary. If we can just take control of those few moments, then we can save ourselves from lifetimes of regret.

Never make a promise when you are happy, never reply when you are angry and never make a decision when you are sad. Procrastinate! If you are patient in one moment of anger, you will escape a hundred days of sorrow.

Focus on the cause

Sometimes it is the environment. If we are in the habit of getting angry, we should try to figure out what is causing that anger. What is the trigger? Unless you focus on the cause, you will not be able to focus on the solution. Sometimes, it might be the environment around us, and then we may have to change it. Take a break. Just like somebody who has boils appearing on his body now and then, our triggers lead us to the cause and one day the solution as well. A doctor will try to heal it from the root by finding out what is causing those boils to appear.

Focus on goals

Try to manage your anger as people cannot manage their stupidity. We all have a friend who is always late for a meeting. Rather than shouting at them, we can focus on what we need to do so they can be on time. Instead of pointing out their faults and spoiling the relationship, we can set a time that is earlier than the actual time to meet. It will make the friend reach on time. This is just one example. Find your goal. Many times parents fight with each other because their child is not behaving properly. Instead of addressing the issue, they get angry. They forget to tell the child what is expected from them. They have not sat down and figured out what it is that they want to see in their child or what they want for their child. Instead of setting goals for their child, they fight. Nobody has communicated properly. I have had to tell such parents to sit down with their children and let them know what is expected from them. If we do not even tell them, how will they know? We keep judging and paralysing ourselves with analysis. So we have to know what we want to accomplish. We have to write it down. Eventually, when we are on the same page, the conflict will get minimized considerably.

Translate your expectations into desires

As I said, proper communication is very important. Saying we would like something is better than saying that we must have it. Turn your demands into requests. Out of false ego, we think we deserve and then we demand. False ego also brings out the worst in the other person. On the other hand, requesting what we want, or what we expect from the other person, resolves the issue to a great extent. Rather than demanding, express it as a request. Humility does not cost us anything. Cultivating this quality will automatically take care of anger.

Focus on the disastrous effects

As I mentioned in the beginning, anger spoils our piety, covers our intelligence, leaves unhealed wounds, and makes us say things we regret forever. We must know that verbal wounds are extremely painful. We should always value our loved ones and not inflict such pain on them through our words. They make us smile, they encourage us to succeed, they lend an ear, they share a word of praise, and they always want to open their hearts to us. But these are the same people we end up hurting the most in our so-called fast-paced life. We tend to forget what others have done for us in our moments of anger. One way to deal with anger is to procrastinate. An extension of that is when you feel anger towards someone, you can start recounting the number of good deeds he has done for you or the amount of contribution that person has made in your life, or the goodness the person has brought into your life. As soon as we shift our focus, we will see that our whole emotional state changes.

Cultivate spiritual strength

Last but not least, try and cultivate spiritual strength. Anger is like an enemy. When an enemy attacks, which it will, we have to fight against it. For this, we need training. If we regularly chant God's name, such as the Hare Krishna mahamantra, read or hear from scriptures like the Bhagavad Gita, Shrimad Bhagavatam, and others associate with saintly people, worship the Lord, we can train our minds to fight against this enemy called rage. Do some simple activities such as offering flowers or fruit or aarti. Worship deities. These are simple things but they give us a lot of spiritual strength. We need physical strength to outpower the external enemy. But what about the internal enemies? To fight against them, we need inner strength. And that inner strength is synonymous with spiritual strength. So if we train ourselves well in advance regularly, we will see our anger subside day by day. Instead of reacting, we will develop the power to respond.

Anger is a disease of the heart and unless we do something to purify the heart, it will not leave us. And the heart gets purified through the process of regular hearing and chanting of God's names, fame, qualities and pastimes from the authorized scriptures such as the Bhagavad Gita, Shrimad Bhagavatam, and Ramayana.

So if we make it a point to regularly hear and chant the glories of the supreme Lord Krishna and His various incarnations in the association of devotees/saintly people, we will see a tremendous change in our consciousness and tolerance levels, and all the divine qualities will manifest. As Shrimad Bhagavatam explains [5.18.12],

yasyasti bhaktir bhagavaty akinchana
sarvair gunais tatra samasate surah
harav abhaktasya kuto mahad-guna
manorathenasati dhavato bahih

'All the demigods and their exalted qualities, such as religion, knowledge and renunciation, become manifest in the body of one who has developed unalloyed devotion for the Supreme Personality of Godhead, Vasudeva. On the other hand, a person devoid of devotional service and engaged in material activities has no good qualities. Even if he is adept at the practice of mystic yoga or the honest endeavor of maintaining his family and relatives, he must be driven by his own mental speculations and must engage in the service of the Lord's external energy. How can there be any good qualities in such a man?'

(When one develops genuine devotion to God or Krishna, gradually all the divine qualities will manifest in their personality. But for somebody who does not have devotion, all their show of good qualities will be lost. It will vanish as soon as there is one provoking situation. Envy, lust, anger, greed, pride and illusion are diseases of the heart. When we incorporate the hearing and chanting processes, the heart gets completely cleansed of all impurities, including anger. And when there is no anger left inside, how will it ever manifest outside? Who will have the power to make us snap?)

Though this cannot be accomplished overnight, every journey starts with a single step. Let us start with one or two or as many of the above solutions and very soon we shall see the desired results. All we need is enthusiasm, determination, patience and His Divine Grace!

IN A NUTSHELL

Plants root from seeds, rice root from crops, anger roots from pain.
The rage that gushes down from the brains to the veins ceases our behaving sane.
Why punish ourselves over a mistake somebody else made?
Consume the medicine of acceptance, let the burning of the soul fade.
Let pain enunciate after the anger goes astray, that way the conversation will aid.
Pray, pray and pray, save yourself from the anger that is no less than a grenade.

CHAPTER 11

KARMA: THE INFALLIBLE JUSTICE

karmano hy api boddhavyam
boddhavyam cha vikarmanah
akarmanashh ca boddhavyam
gahana karmano gatih

—Bhagavad Gita [4.17]

(The intricacies of karma/action are very hard to understand. Therefore, one should know properly what action is, what forbidden action is, and what inaction is.)

We have the best of intentions and yet we are misunderstood. We put in our best efforts, yet we fail. We work hard for happiness and still major setbacks come in our lives. Why? The one word and a very common answer is 'karma'. But what exactly is karma? How does it act? Can we do something about it?

Questions like these are much more common today than a few decades ago. This is evident from the fact that not only has the word 'karma' found its place in the English dictionary, but also Gallup polls* show an increase in the percentage of people, not only in the Eastern world but also in the Western world, who believe in karma. However, karma is not just a belief system; it is a precise science. Even more important is that it is a science of consequences. Consequences that we have to bear in our lives (as the present one is not the only life we have). Therefore, it is vital to understand this science.

THE LOGIC

The law of karma is: for every action, there is an equal and opposite reaction. In the Bible, it is phrased as: As you sow, so shall you reap.

Science has discovered that all of nature obeys laws. Science is nothing but a study and application of nature's laws. If all of nature is governed by laws, why should we humans be an exception to such laws?

There is a saying: we can never break God's laws; we can only break ourselves against God's laws. If somebody says, 'I do not believe in the law of gravity' and jumps from the top of a ten-storey building, what will happen? They will not break the law of gravity but break themselves against the law. Similarly,

---

* Gallup, Inc. is an American analytics and advisory company based in Washington, D.C. Founded by George Gallup in 1935, the company became known for its public opinion polls conducted worldwide.

we can never break any of the laws of God. But just as the law of gravity is impartial and inexorable and acts on all physical objects indiscriminately, the law of karma is impartial and acts on all living entities indiscriminately.

As humans, we are blessed with a special facility that no other species possess: the ability to make choices. And as we have this special boon, we are also held responsible for the choices we make. When more is given, more is expected too.

WHAT IS THE NEED?

Any amount of distress we go through in life is the result of our past karmas.

Thus, understanding the science of Karma helps us make sense of the injustice we suffer in this life and understand why different people have different starting points in life. Someone is born poor while someone is born with a silver spoon in their mouth. Someone is healthy and someone is plagued with diseases. Someone is born beautiful whereas someone is not. Someone works hard but fails to achieve the desired result and someone just dances their way to success with ease, sometimes even with manipulation. When we do not understand the laws of karma properly, it can lead to utter confusion, shock and non-acceptance of reality, which aggravates the suffering.

RESPONSE TO SETBACKS

Because they have no or little knowledge, different people respond in different ways when something goes wrong. Most common is to blame God.

Response type one: deism

Harold Kushner was a rabbi. His only son developed progeria at the age of seven. Progeria is a disease where the person starts aging prematurely. The son died at the age of fourteen. Kushner had preached about religion and God all his life but did not have any knowledge of karma and its laws. Therefore, when his son passed away, he was extremely upset and wanted to defy Him. But he could not do it outrightly. How could he suddenly convince people the opposite of what he had made them believe all his life? So, very intelligently, he struck a compromise. He wrote a book called *When Bad Things Happen to Good People*. In this book, he presented God as someone who had faults and was not as great as people believed. He brought God down to a very ordinary level, on a mundane platform, and wrote, 'God may be all-powerful and all-knowing, but He is not all-merciful. Otherwise, He would have forgiven my child and saved him'. He believed that a powerful God would have been able to protect an innocent kid who could not have done any wrong at such a young age. And because he was angry, he demeaned God and presented Him as flawed.

Response type two: atheism

Some people turn into die-hard atheists when something goes wrong since they cannot come to terms with reality. They cannot accept the outcome as it's opposite to their wishes, and stay in denial. This sort of denial ultimately leads to the denial of the existence of God.

Response type three: confusion

Years ago in Scotland, one Clark family had a dream. Clark and his wife worked and saved, making plans for their nine children and themselves to travel to the US. It had taken years, but they had finally saved enough money and had got passports and reservations for the whole family on a new liner sailing to the US.

The entire family was filled with anticipation and excitement about their new life. However, seven days before their departure, the youngest son was bitten by a dog. The doctor sewed up the little boy but hung a yellow sheet on the Clarks' front door. Because of the possibility of rabies, they were being quarantined for fourteen days.

The family's dreams were dashed. They would not be able to make the trip to the US as they had planned. The father, filled with disappointment and anger, stomped to the dock to watch the ship sail without the Clark family on it. The father shed tears of disappointment and cursed both his son and God for their misfortune. Five days later, the tragic news spread throughout Scotland; the mighty *Titanic* had sunk, taking hundreds of lives with it. The Clark family was to be on that ship, but because the son had been bitten by a dog, they escaped. When Mr Clark heard the news, he hugged his son and thanked him for saving the family. He thanked God for saving their lives and turning what he had felt was a tragedy into a blessing.

Even God must have been confused. One week ago He was being criticized and one week later He was being thanked for the same act.

THE NEED FOR THE LAW

To maintain order

Imagine a city with no rules. It would be chaotic. We are expected to follow certain laws. And when we do not, a reaction must come. The government creates amenities, such as roads and hospitals, for our benefit and also expects us not to abuse those facilities or trouble others who are entitled to use them. If we do not abide by the laws, the same government that provided us with all these facilities would punish us.

To train us

If the students study well, their parents appreciate them and give them gifts. If they do not study, they are chastised. Wherever there is a superior supervisor, the normal way of training is punishment for the bad and reward for the good. Similarly, since God is the most benevolent parent and the most intelligent trainer, he also follows the same system. He uses the law of karma to train us.

Three types of karmas

The Bhagavad Gita (4.17) mentions,

karmano hy api boddhavyam
boddhavyam cha vikarmanaḥ
akarmanash cha boddhavyaṁ
gahana karmano gatih

(The intricacies of karma/action are very hard to understand. Therefore, one should know properly what action [karma] is, what forbidden action [vikarma] is and what inaction [akarma] is.)

Karma, in a stricter, scriptural sense, primarily means the actions done under one's prescribed duties as mentioned in the scriptures. In contrast to karma, there is vikarma, which refers to actions done contrary to the scriptures by the misuse of one's free will. Vikarma degrades one's intelligence, takes one down to the lower forms of life and creates future suffering. The present yuga is full of vikarma, and the four main vikarmic activities or the four pillars of adharma are intoxication, meat-eating, gambling and illicit sex. These four main irreligious activities lead to severe karmic reactions, which manifest both in future and in present lives.

What starts with 'cheers!' often leads to cheerless repercussions.

Different from karma and vikarma is akarma. Akarma does not mean inactivity, but an activity that brings no reaction, that frees one from the reactions to past actions, and eventually the cycle of birth and death. Essentially, activities concerning God, the supreme judge.

WHERE DOES IT BEGIN?

If there is an effect, there must be a cause too, though the cause might not always be visible. Once we understand the intricacies of karma (how it acts and when it starts), we can also understand how it ends. Unless we understand the cause, how can we take care of the effect?

ORIGINALLY WE ARE THE RESIDENTS OF THE SPIRITUAL WORLD

The Bhagavad Gita [2.11–30] mentions that we are spirit souls or spiritual beings and not these material bodies. Thus, the spiritual world is our real home. Just like how there are heavenly planets, hellish planets and the middle planetary system of which our earth is a tiny part, there are spiritual planets as well much beyond the realm of the material world we live in and that is where we belong. Even if someone says that they do not believe in such things, we cannot deny the fact that we will have to leave this world and the soul has to go somewhere. And that somewhere could be any of the above-mentioned realms depending on what we desire and work towards.

When someone passes away, are we not wondering whether the soul has gone to a better place? Thus subconsciously we all believe in the higher realms. But if we are the residents of the spiritual world, what are we doing in this messy material world full of uncertainties? How did we end up here?

Well! The answer is given in Chaitanya Charitamrita Madhya Lila [20.117],

nadia bhuli' sei jiva nadi-bahirmukha
ataeva maya tare deya saṁsara-duhkha

(When the living entity forgets his constitutional position as an eternal servant of Krishna or God, he is immediately entrapped by the illusory, external energy called Maya. Therefore the illusory energy gives him all kinds of misery in his material existence.)

Also, in Prema-vivarta [6.2], it says

Krishna bhuliya jiva bhoga vancha kare
pashate maya tare japatiya dhare

(When an individual soul forgets his eternal relationship with Krishna and tries to lord it over the material nature or resources, that condition, that forgetful condition, is called maya, or illusion.)

As soon as a particular soul desires to live a life independent of God, the soul is sent to the material world, the world of maya or illusion, because in the spiritual world where everyone cooperates with the will of God, there is complete harmony and it cannot be allowed to be disrupted. Any desire which is separate from God is called material desire. And to fulfil material desires, we have to come to the material world, that is, the world of matter.

The Bible talks of a similar principle through the story of Adam and Eve. God gave them heaven, nice gardens, palaces, and trees full of fruits, and said that everything was there for them to enjoy. However, He instructed them to not eat apple from a particular tree.

The forbidden is tempting. It is the human tendency that if we tell someone not to do something, that is the only thing they want to do. If we give our phone to someone and tell him not to open WhatsApp, the person's whole consciousness will be fixed on WhatsApp only. Adam and Eve ended up eating that apple. Till then they moved around naked; there was no conception of I, me and mine, male or female. They were on the spiritual platform, which is a platform of equality. But the material platform is a platform of duality; happiness–distress, honour–dishonour, male–female, friend–enemy. As soon as they ate the apple, dualities of male and female arose in their minds and they started covering themselves; they became restless and all miseries and anxieties followed them. What exactly was the problem here? The problem was not that they ate the apple. Apples are good; whether it is a phone or a fruit! The problem was disobedience. They disobeyed God's instructions and immediately all the effective dualities began bothering them.

Disobedience to the will or laws of God is the root cause of the bondage of karmic reactions. As soon as we disobey, we come under the control of the laws of karma, our freedom is checked, and we face impediments in life. Just like the laws in a city or a state: those who follow the laws live happily but the freedom of those who disobey is curtailed so that innocent citizens of the city can live peacefully in complete harmony.

So the soul has come down from 'vaikuntha' (the spiritual world), a place free from misery to 'kuntha' (the material world), the world of misery, a prison house.

What happens now?

Another name for the material world is 'karagar' or a 'prison house'. And who is sent to a prison house? Those who act against the will of the government. So those who desire to act against God's will are sent to this prison house for rectification.

A jail or a prison house must have a jailor.

Another name for the material world is 'durg'. And the jailor for this 'durg' is Goddess Durga. Hence the name. She is in charge of rectifying rebellious souls.

Whom does the law punish? Somebody who refuses to obey it. The government laws are there to protect us but the same laws will punish us when we rebel. When we are in this material world, there are different miseries we have to go through. Goddess Durga has the thankless task of inflicting threefold miseries upon reckless souls. These are: miseries caused by mind and body; miseries caused by other living entities such as our friends, relatives, colleagues, viruses and bacteria; and then there are miseries caused by natural disasters. Durga is a mother but has to perform this duty. A jailor may not like to punish the prisoners, but he has to do his duty to rectify them.

The sufferings we are made to endure are meant to serve as an impetus to develop a desire for the world free from miseries, that is, the spiritual world or vaikuntha, as much as the punishments in the prison house are meant to create a desire in the heart to get out and never break the law again. However, the good news is that this suffering is not eternal.

What can we do now?

When does a criminal get relief from the punishments of the government? When he is willing to give up his separatist mentality. When does Goddess Durga stop inflicting punishments upon us? As soon as she sees that we are now beginning to give up our rebellion towards God and working towards becoming more and more God-conscious. Thus we worship God, remember Him, and chant His names, not for His benefit but for our benefit.

The prisoner may be sentenced to ten years of imprisonment but when they start rectifying their behaviour inside the jail, they may be pardoned and released within five years. Therefore, it does not matter how much karma we have carried from the past. We can be pardoned.

If in the ordinary material world, the head of the state can have such powers to pardon a criminal or reduce their sentence, why do we think God cannot nullify our karmic reactions? In essence, the law of karma starts when we decide to live a life independent of God and it ends when we give up that independence and increase our dependence on Him by obeying His laws.

THE GREATEST NEED

We think that by being independent, we will be happy. But think logically. Who enjoys the most? And who suffers? Those who follow the laws of the state or those who rebel against the state? We need to stop living our life according to our whims and fancies and start living in harmony with the will of God. People often suggest, 'Oh! Whatever makes you feel good, just do that! Whatever makes you happy, just do that!' If everybody lived their life their way, then what is the difference between us and other species? 'Just do it' because it feels good without understanding the repercussions is foolish and the philosophy of the lower species. But they can afford to do it because unlike us, they do not have the free will to choose and, hence, do not get reactions to their karmas like us humans. But we are accountable for our actions and must pay the consequences.

The law of karma takes into consideration not just one lifetime but all the lifetimes. Life is a multi-innings game. It is a test match, not a one-day. Everything is taken into consideration and that is why people have different starting points in life.

Suppose we do not know what a test match is and watch one. We see one team getting all out after scoring 250 runs. The other team comes in to bat and their starting score is 305.

So if we lack knowledge about cricket, we will conclude this to be unjust. So at this point in time, we need a person who has the knowledge to tell us, 'This is a multi-innings game. Their starting point is 305 because they have already played an innings before.'

But the important thing is, as human beings, it does not matter how badly we have played our previous innings. If we play well in the present innings, we can still win. That is the blessing the Lord has bestowed upon human beings. Again and again, the scriptures proclaim how human life is so special, so rare. To end the cycle of karma, to end the cycle of birth and death, and to achieve liberation is only possible in human life.

We do not necessarily have to go through our karma. We can do something to counteract them. Free will is given to all human beings, and by making the right choices, we can make sure that we do not suffer or go through any misery in the future. Karma manifests as legal implications, chronic diseases, mental distress, and so on at different intervals. Some of the karma has already fructified and we have received reactions in the past. Some are fructifying now and some will fructify in the future. So we do not know how much is in store. What do we do now?

THE WAY OUT

Stop sinning

When we need to get cured of an acute disease, the first thing we need to do is stop doing what made us sick in the first place. We must choose carefully, but our choices about right and wrong should be based on the scriptures. We must know what is right and do what is right. Right is right even if no one does it and wrong is wrong even if everyone does it. So we must be intelligent enough to discriminate, without falling prey to others' opinions.

Atonement

Shrimad Bhagavatam [6.1.7] states

shri-shuka uvacha
na ched ihaivapachitim yathamhasah
kritasya kuryan mana-ukta-panibhih
dhruvam sa vai pretya narakan upaiti
ye kirtita me bhavatas tigma-yatanah

(Shukadeva Gosvami replied, 'My dear king, if before one's next death whatever impious acts one has performed in this life with his mind, words and body are not counteracted through proper atonement according to the description of the Manu-samhita and other dharma-sastras, one will certainly enter the hellish planets after death and undergo terrible suffering, as I have previously described to you.')

The Vedic scriptures prescribe various processes of atonement that every human being must perform before the hour of death arrives so that future suffering can be avoided. However, the defect with these processes is that they might nullify the sinful reactions but not the sinful mentality. The seeds of sinful desires still stay. As long as the sinful inclination stays, a person will again commit a forbidden act and create suffering for himself. It is like the bathing of an elephant. An elephant takes a nice bath but throws dirt all over its body again as soon as it comes out of the water.

Bhakti yoga (devotional service)

Only through the process of devotional service of Krishna(God) do we become free, not just from sinful karmas but also from the habit or inclination to sin. Krishna is the supreme autocrat and can change a person's destiny as and when He wants, if He is pleased with us. And the only thing that pleases Him is bhakti or the process of devotional service. The Shrimad Bhagavatam [6.1.15 16, 1819] states

kechit kevalaya bhaktya
asudeva-parayanah
agham dhunvanti kartsnyena
niharam iva bhaskarah

(Only a rare person who has adopted complete, unalloyed devotional service to Krishna can uproot the weeds of sinful actions with no possibility that they will revive. He can do this simply by discharging devotional service, just as the sun can immediately dissipate fog with its rays.)

na tatha hy aghavan rajan
puyeta tapa-adibhih
yatha krishnarpita-pranas
tat-purusha-nishevaya

(My dear King, if a sinful person engages in the service of a bona fide devotee of the Lord and thus learns how to dedicate his life unto the lotus feet of Krishna, he can be completely purified. One cannot be purified merely by undergoing austerity, penance, brahmacharya and the other methods of atonement I have previously described.)

prayashchittani cirnani
ajendra-paranmukham
na nishpunanti ajendra
sura-kumbham ivapagah

(My dear King, as a pot containing liquor cannot be purified even if washed in the waters of many rivers, non-devotees cannot be purified by processes of atonement even if they perform them very well.)

sakrin manah rishna-padaravindayor
niveshitaṁ tad-guna-ragi yair iha
na te yamaṁ pasha-bhritash cha tad-bhatan
svapne 'pi pashyanti hi chirna-nishkritah

(Although not having fully realized Krishna, persons who have even once surrendered completely unto His lotus feet and who have become attracted to His name, form, qualities and pastimes are completely freed of all sinful reactions, for they have thus accepted the true method of atonement. Even in dreams, such surrendered souls do not see Yamaraj or his order carriers, who are equipped with ropes to bind the sinful.)

Lord Brahma, the first-created being, explains in Sri Brahma-samhita [5.54]

karmani nirdahati kintu cha bhakti-bhajam
govindam adi-purusham tam aham bhajami

(I adore the primeval Lord Govinda (Krishna), who burns up to their roots all fruitive karmas of those who are imbued with devotion.)

Lord Krishna's other name is Mukunda (the giver of mukti or liberation from the bondage of karmas). Anyone can say anything but Lord Brahma's opinion must be accepted as authoritative as he is the creator and certainly knows more than any of us. Lord Krishna personally gives the assurance in the Bhagavad Gita [18.66] in His supreme instruction

sarva-dharman parityajya
mam ekam sharanam vraja
aham tvam sarva-papebhyo
mokshayishyami ma suchah

(Abandon all varieties of religion and just surrender unto Me. I shall deliver you from all sinful reactions. Do not fear.)

A prisoner cannot free himself but the head of the state can. Similarly, on our own, it is impossible to be freed. But the Lord, out of His supreme kindness, can set us free if we engage in His devotional service.

But how to do it? How do we take shelter?

Devotional service or bhakti has nine limbs:

- Hearing (shravanam) about the Lord's names, forms, qualities, and pastimes from the scriptures such as the Bhagavad Gita and Shrimad Bhagavatam
- Chanting the holy names
- Remembering (Vishnu smaranam)
- Serving the Lord's lotus feet (pada sevanam)
- Deity worship (archanam)
- Praying (vandanam)
- Executing orders (dasyam)

- Serving as a friend (sakhyam)
- Complete surrender (atma nivedanam)—offering everything that we have in His service

Any of the above practices we accept daily can gradually free us from karmic reactions and purify our hearts, thus bringing us closer to God more and more. However living in today's day and age where we hardly seem to have any time, we want the quickest, safest, surest and easiest way. And that means chanting the Lord's holy names as per Chaitanya Charitamrita, Antya [4.70-1]

bhajanera madhye shreshtha nava-vidha bhakti
'krishna-prema,' 'krishna' dite dhare maha-shakti
tara madhye sarva-shreshthha nama-sankirtana
niraparadhe nama laile paya prema-dhana

(Of all the different spiritual practices, the nine forms of bhakti (sravanam, kirtanam, and others) are the best because they have great potency to deliver Krishna and ecstatic love and devotion for Him. Of these nine practices, nama-sankirtana (chanting or singing of His names) is the best. By chanting the holy name without offense, one very easily obtains the priceless treasure of love for Krishna and thus surpasses the jurisdiction of Karma.)

Krishna has appeared in Kaliyuga as His name.

kali-kale nama-rupe krishna-avatara
nama haite haya sarva-jagat-nistara

(In this Age of Kali, the holy name of the Lord, the Hare Krishna mahamantra, is the incarnation of Lord Krishna. Simply by chanting the holy name, one associates with the Lord directly. Anyone who does this is certainly liberated (of his karmas).)

The following references from various authorized scriptures further endorse the fact. The Brihan-Naradiya Purana says

harer nama harer nama, harer namaiva kevalam
alua nasty eva nasty eva, nasty eva gatir anyatha

(In this age of quarrel and hypocrisy, the only means of deliverance is the chanting of the holy names of the Lord. There is no other way.)

Shrimad Bhagavatam [1.1.14] says

apannah samsritim ghoram
yan-nama vivasho grinan
tatah sadyo vimuchyeta
yad bibheti svayam bhayam

(Living beings who are entangled in the complicated meshes of birth and death can be freed immediately by even unconsciously chanting the holy name of Krishna, which is feared by fear personified.)

The Shrimad Bhagavatam [6.2.14] explains

sanketyam parihasyam va
stobham helanam eva va
vaikuntha-nama-grahanam
assheshagha-haram viduh

(One who chants the holy name of the Lord is immediately freed from the reactions of unlimited sinful karmas, even if he chants indirectly [to indicate something else], jokingly, for musical entertainment, or even neglectfully. This is accepted by all the learned scholars of the scriptures.)

The Shrimad Bhagavatam [6.2.18] says

ajnanad athava jnanad
uttamashloka-nama yat
sankirtitam agham pumso
dahed edho yathanalah

(As a fire burns dry grass to ashes, so the holy name of the Lord, whether chanted knowingly or unknowingly, burns to ashes, without fail, all the reactions of one's sinful karmas.)

Fire will act, regardless of whether handled by an innocent child or by someone well aware of its power. For example, if a field of straw or dry grass is set afire, either by an elderly man who knows the power of fire or by a child who does not, the grass will be burnt to ashes. Similarly, one may or may not know the power of chanting the holy name of Krishna, the Hare Krishna mahamantra, but if one chants he will become free from all sinful reactions. In the Shrimad Bhagavatam [6.3.31], it is said,

tasmat sankirtanam vishnor
jagan-mangalam amhasam
ahatma api kauravya
viddhy aikantika-nishkritam

(Shukadeva Gosvami continued: My dear King, the chanting of the holy name of the Lord can uproot even the reactions of the greatest sins. Therefore the chanting of the sankirtana movement is the most auspicious activity in the entire universe. Please try to understand this so that others will take it seriously.)

The Kali-santarana Upanishad from Krishna Yajur Veda explains

hare krishna hare krishna krishna krishna hare hare
hare rama hare rama rama rama hare hare
iti sodasakam namnam kali-kalmasa-nasanam
natah parataropayah sarva-vedesu drsyate

(Lord Brahma to Narada: The sixteen names of the Hare Krishna mahamantra—Hare Krishna Hare Krishna, Krishna Krishna Hare Hare; Hare Rama Hare Rama, Rama Rama Hare Hare—destroy all the inauspiciousness of Kaliyuga. This is the conclusion of all the Vedas.)

There are countless such verses and references in the Vedic scriptures regarding the power of the holy names of Krishna in destroying a person's sinful karmas.

It is the easiest process and can be practiced even by a child. It can also be practiced anywhere and at any time. One can chant before or after taking a bath, sitting or while walking. There are no hard and fast rules. The only condition is that when we chant, we should try to hear the sound of the mantra.

The Shrimad Bhagavatam, sixth canto (Chapters 1 to 3), talks about a person named Ajamil who spent his entire life committing all kinds of sinful acts. Somehow, by some unimaginable good fortune, he named his youngest son, to whom he was most attached, Narayan. When Ajamil was on his deathbed, three ferocious messengers of Yamaraj (the universal judge) came to take him to their master for punishment. When Ajamil saw them, he became very frightened and in a helpless state called out to his son (who was playing close by). 'Narayan!' he cried, and instantly the room was lit up with the appearance and divine effulgence of four Vishnudutas, the messengers of Lord Narayan. In resounding voices, they stopped the Yamadutas from taking Ajamil with them. They even cut off the ropes the Yamadutas had bound Ajamil with.

For the first time, the Yamadutas faced a strange situation where they were prevented from doing their duty. When they questioned as to why they were trying to protect a sinful soul like Ajamil, the Vishnudutas smiled and replied (Shrimad Bhagavatam 6.2.7),

ayam hi krita-nirvesho
anma-koty-amhasam api
yad vyajahara vivasho
nama svasty-ayanam hareh

(Ajamil has already atoned for all his sinful actions. Indeed, he has atoned not only for sins performed in one life but for those performed in millions of lives, for in a helpless condition he chanted the holy name of Narayana. Even though he did not chant purely, he chanted without offense, and therefore he is now pure and eligible for liberation.)

In this regard, the great Vaishnava acharya Shrila Vishvanatha Chakravarti Thakura quotes the following verses from the Brihad-Vishnu Purana,

namno hi yavati shaktih
papa-nirharane hareh
tavat kartum na shaknoti
patakam pataki narah

(Simply by chanting one holy name of Hari, a sinful man can counteract the reactions to more sins than he is able to commit.)

The Garuda Purana says

avashenapi yan-namni
kirtite sarva-patakaih
puman vimuchyate sadyah
simha-trastair mrigair iva

(If one chants the holy name of the Lord, even in a helpless condition or without desiring to do so, all the reactions of his sinful life depart, just as when a lion roars, all the small animals flee in fear.)

In the Skanda Purana, it is said

sakrid uccaritam yena
harir ity akshara-dvayam
baddha-parikaras tena
mokshaya gamanam prati

(By once chanting the holy name of the Lord, which consists of the two syllables *ha-ri,* one guarantees his path to liberation.)

Thus Ajamil was eventually saved and given a second chance. After experiencing the power of the Lord's name, he retired to Haridwar and chanted day and night, but this time, with a heart full of gratitude. Through meditations on the sound and power of the Lord's name, he was purified and when his destined moment to leave this world came, the same four Vishnudutas, his saviours, came in a divine airplane and took him to the spiritual world in the presence of Lord Narayan to live a life of eternal happiness.

The creation of the Lord is complete and there is no loophole. If there are problems, there are solutions too. In the Bhagavad Gita [8.15], Krishna described this world as 'duhkhalayam' (a place of misery) and 'ashashvatam' (temporary). However, we do not need to be miserable. We want to be happy and what stops us from becoming happy? Problems. And why do problems occur? Because of past karmas. And the devotional service (beginning with hearing and chanting) to Lord Krishna, the supremely independent Lord not bound by any rules, can counteract all types of Karmic reactions, thus destroying the root cause of all our miseries and eventually bringing us back to the spiritual world, our real home where we belong, where there is no misery, no old age, no death and no diseases. The realm where life is eternal and full of bliss. And the realm where we will be reunited with our eternal father and mother, Radha and Krishna, to attain eternal happiness. So chant 'Hare Krishna Hare Krishna, Krishna Krishna Hare Hare; Hare Rama Hare Rama, Rama Rama Hare Hare' and watch miracles unfold.

IN A NUTSHELL

It's true that every ball bounces back, what goes around comes around.

Be prudent about your action, be aware, there will always be a reaction.

The Earth is round, the act of wounding others leads to karma being astound.

Chant to be purified, let the Lord grease the wheels to repudiate karma that is demoralized.

Spirituality is the most poignant cleanser, all you have to do is surrender.

It is now or never, climb Krishna's chariot of spirituality and press the lever.

CHAPTER 12

DEATH: THE INEVITABLE REALITY

In life, one thing is absolutely certain: death. According to the Bhagavad Gita [2.27]

jatasya hi dhruvo mrityur
dhruvam janma mritasya cha
tasmad apariharye 'rthe
na tvam sochitum arhasi

(One who has taken his birth is sure to die, and after death one is sure to take birth again. Therefore, in the unavoidable discharge of your duty, you should not lament.)

From the moment we are born, we are, in a sense, dying, and the sooner we realize how impermanent this life is, the less entangled we will be in superficial things that bring pain to our hearts. Death is a very essential topic for everyone to think about because it is a subject that specifically and directly involves us, as well as everyone near and dear to us. It is the inevitable conclusion of what we know to be life and this subject matter of death has always been a great mystery. The thought of it is painful, fearful and unacceptable.

In the great epic the Mahabharata ('Van Parva'), during the dialogue between Yaksha and King Yudhishthira, one of the questions asked was, 'What is the most wonderful or the most astonishing thing in this world?' King Yudhishthira had replied, 'Death. Every day numerous living entities are dying and going to the abode of Yama (the Lord of death). Yet one thinks and believes one will live forever. What can be more wonderful than this?'

Throughout our lives, we are endeavouring to solve the problems that face us, but there is one problem that is universal to every one of us. Through all science and technology, we have no solution to this problem and that is the problem of death. 'Sure as death' is a saying signifying that we all must meet that fate today or tomorrow. So must all those whom we love (or hate).

WHAT HAPPENS IN DEATH?

Everyone in this world has a fixed duration of life to spend. It is decided at the time of birth itself. As soon as that duration is over, everyone must leave. No one can prolong a person's life even for a moment. The immediate reason could be disease or accidents, but the ultimate reason is that our fixed time is over.

The Garuda Purana explains how the pain experienced at the time of death is equivalent to the pain caused by forty thousand scorpions biting simultaneously. It is an excruciatingly painful experience. Imagine we have been living in a house for a long time and suddenly we are asked or forced to vacate. We would be devastated due to the attachment we have developed with our house. Similarly, the soul, while living in the body for years becomes attached to it and, thus, feels the pain when it has to leave at the destined moment. No one wants to die but no one can avoid it.

WHAT HAPPENS AFTER DEATH?

This world is characterized by change. Nothing is permanent. It is a world of matter and anything made of matter must have a shelf life. Things are constantly changing and death is simply the final change.

Lord Krishna explains in the Bhagavad Gita [2.13],

dehino 'smin yatha dehe
kaumaram yauvanam jara
tatha dehantara-praptir
dhiras tatra na muhyati

(As the embodied soul continuously passes, in this body, from boyhood to youth to old age, the soul similarly passes into another body at death. A sober person is not bewildered by such a change.)

The body starts dying as soon as we are born. It goes through six changes: it is born, grows, stays, produces by-products, dwindles and dies. So there is a change happening every moment and death is simply the final change. After death, the soul enters another body depending on the consciousness cultivated and the karmas in the past life.

We have three bodies: one, the gross body that everyone can see; two, the subtle body consisting of three subtle elements: the mind, intelligence and false ego; and three, the spiritual body or the soul.

When a person dies, the gross body is left behind, but the soul is carried to the next destination based on desires and thoughts, especially at the last moment. Lord Krishna clearly explains in the Bhagavad Gita [8.6] the factor that decides where the soul is going,

yam yam vapi smaran bhavam
tyajaty ante kalevaram
tam tam evaiti kaunteya
sada tad-bhava-bhavitah

(Whatever state of being one remembers when he quits his body, O son of Kunti, that state he will attain without fail.)

Thus our next body, family, and place of birth are decided as per our last thoughts and our last thoughts will be related to things we have throughout our life. Therefore it is said, 'Life is a preparation. Death done is the examination'.

How well or badly we have lived our life will be tested at the time of death. It is the final exam. And we all know when we go to a school or college, the final exam carries the maximum weightage. Small unit tests are held regularly throughout the semester, but the purpose of these is to prepare us for the final test. Similarly, all the trials and tests that come into our life are simply meant to remind that there will be a final test and we better get serious.

DEATH: THE FINAL EXAM! BUT WHY?

The moments before death decide whether we are going to a better place, remain stuck in the same place, or get a lower realm or form. Death is a crucial moment in a person's life. We should not only learn the art of living but also the art of dying. The latter is even more important.

When we pass the final exam, we are promoted. Similarly, we are promoted to the highest destination if we can answer the final exam in the right way. And what is the right way or what decides whether our human life has been a success? The answer is in the Shrimad Bhagavatam [2.1.6] is

etavan sankhya-yogabhyam
sva-dharma-parinishthaya
aray-labhah parah pumsam
ante arayana-smritih

(The highest perfection of human life, achieved either by complete knowledge of matter and spirit, by the practice of mystic powers, or by perfect discharge of occupational duty, is to remember the personality of the Godhead at the end of life.)

Human life is meant to put an end to the cycle of birth and death forever. It is only possible if we can remember the Lord at the last moment. If we remember Him, we go to His abode, the supremely blissful spiritual world. But if we remember anything or anyone else, we stay stuck in the material world, full of miseries, wherein repeated birth and death take place.

Thus death is the most important exam. Whatever we have done throughout our life will be tested at the moment of death similar to how we are tested during the final exam. Hence, we can decide if we want to study during the semester or miss the opportunity to prepare for it.

Thus when someone is about to pass away, we must try and create an atmosphere around them to enhance the remembrance of the Lord. We can play or personally chant the names of the Lord, recite Gita or Shrimad Bhagavatam, or fill the room with pictures of Lord Krishna/Lord Rama/ Lord Vishnu.

WHY DO WE NEVER WISH TO DIE?

We all are eternal spirit souls and we are used to eternal life. In this material world where everything must perish after some time, we will also experience death. The material body that is given to us when we come here is what truly dies. As we are so attached to this body and identify with it, whenever something happens to it, we feel it is happening to us. However, we do not die. Rather we just move into another body once this body becomes unfit for living. Death is the end of everything that we feel makes us happy and as eternally blissful souls, parts and parcels of God, we are not used to it. Thus, death feels like an unnatural phenomenon to us and is utterly unacceptable.

HOW TO DEAL WITH IT?

Dealing with death could be both stressful and painful. It is inevitable and we cannot escape it, no matter who we are. Hence, we can focus on something we do to lessen the pain or turn it into a stepping stone to something better rather than a roadblock.

Pain is inevitable. Suffering is optional.

Here are a few tips when dealing with the death of another person.

Acceptance

Not every problem in the world has a solution. Some problems can be solved whereas some just need to be accepted and tolerated. Lord Krishna tells in the Bhagavad Gita [2.14],

matra-sparshas tu kaunteya
shitoshna-sukha-duhkha-dah
agamapayino 'nityas
tams titikshasva bharata

(O son of Kunti, the non-permanent appearance of happiness and distress, and their disappearance in due course, are like the appearance and disappearance of winter and summer seasons. They arise from sense perception, O scion of Bharata, and one must learn to tolerate them without being disturbed.)

When someone passes away, we aggravate our suffering and refuse to accept what has happened. The denial of reality hurts more than the reality itself.

Acceptance reduces our pain a lot. Acceptance becomes easier when we learn to see this world through the eyes of the scriptures. The scriptures are like guidebooks to help us navigate every stage of our life, be it good or bad. They teach us how nothing in this world is permanent. When we start accepting the eternal reality that everyone who is born will die sooner or later, it helps us make peace with the situation. A wonderful story illustrates this point so beautifully.

A famous saint was staying in a village. A woman came to him, crying and screaming. Her only child had suddenly passed away. The whole village was affected by her grief and followed her. The saint's disciples were also affected. They started praying for the guru to bless the child so that he would come back to life.

The saint remained silent. He looked at the dead child and then looked at the desperate, crying mother and told her, 'Don't cry! Just do one thing and your child will be back. I need a bowl of rice to revive your child. So go back to the village and get me one, but from a house where no one has ever died.'

The woman was overjoyed. She ran to the village. She went from one family to another, asking for a bowl of rice but each family would agree initially and then decline on hearing the condition. She went on asking until she had gone to every house in the village.

Gradually, the woman understood the meaning of the saint's condition. The realization finally dawned on her that no place existed in the world, forget her village, where death had not taken someone. She was asking for the inevitable. As soon as she began to accept the reality, her tears dried and suddenly she experienced an inexplicable peace inside her. She realized that whoever is born will have to die. It is only a question of years. Some will die sooner, others later, but death is inevitable. She came back and thanked the saint for this realization.

Thus, the first step towards healing of any kind is 'acceptance'.

Change the vibe

We are blessed with the ability to make choices, and we have a choice not to lament. When someone passes away, we have two choices: to either keep crying or to do something for the benefit of the soul which has left us. Any sensible person would choose the second option. We are human beings and do feel hurt, but if we focus on 'what can we do now?' instead of 'why did it happen?' we will be in a better position to handle the situation.

We should tell ourselves, 'All right! This has happened now. I cannot undo it. But what is the best thing I can do in this situation to make it better? How can I help the soul?' As soon as we shift our focus to the solution, we will feel more positive and will be doing something worthwhile.

So the negative vibe created by the passing away must be replaced by the divine vibe. Instead of simply lamenting, we must start chanting the Lord's holy names (such as the Hare Krishna mahamantra), recite the Bhagavad Gita, Shrimad Bhagavatam and the Ramayana. The divine sound of the Lord's names and words will certainly intervene and counteract all negativity.

I have experienced the power of this method on various occasions.

Once I received a call from the member of a dear family that one of the elders of the family had passed away and if I could come over with a few devotees for kirtan (singing of the Lord's holy names). I immediately rushed. As soon as I reached their home, it did not feel that death had touched it. It felt like a holy festival was taking place. The reason was this: it was a tradition in the family that as soon as someone passed away, all the family members and relatives came together and started the recitation of the Gita, Ramayana, Shrimad Bhagavatam, circumambulation of Tulasi and kirtans. The family members would take turns in twelve and twenty-four hour kirtans. The result: the overall vibe of the place became most divine. The members of the family had no time for lamentation. They felt positive and most importantly the soul that had passed away received tremendous spiritual credits due to which its onwards journey got most comfortable.

When we simply lament, the journey of the soul gets impeded and it is not happy with it. Thus our true love for the soul is not expressed by crying but by doing something to better their condition and that is only possible by invoking the Lord's presence into the situation through His name, remembrance and glorification. By doing this, we feel better and the soul that passed away attains a higher and a better destination.

So do not just cry. Do something better to change the vibe and help the soul!

Fear of our death

Honestly speaking, we are so busy with our fast-paced life that we do not even care. We do not realize that death can come at any moment. We live in a place where there is danger at every step. We see so many people dying but still, it does not occur to us that we will also meet the same fate one day. When that day will come, we do not know. But it will, sooner or later.

But then should we be paranoid and give up living our life or start living in constant fear? No! That is not what it means. It simply means that while enjoying our life, we must not forget about the final exam. We should not forget that this human life is valuable and must not be wasted simply in material pursuits. It has been given mainly for self-realization and to seek answers to questions such as 'Who am I? Where do I come from? Where will I go? What is the purpose of life? Who is God? What is my relationship with Him? How can I revive that relationship? Why do I suffer even when I do not want to?' We can try and accomplish our material goals without forgetting the ultimate goal. And the ultimate goal is to reach the highest place, the spiritual world, which is our real home.

But how can we expect to achieve this if we do not even pay attention to the uncertainty of life and the final exam that we all are expected to pass to achieve perfection in human life?

The final exam must come. So what should we do?

PREPARE!

If we anticipate something, we must get ready to deal with it.

When we realize there is an exam, the most important one, we start preparing. And when do we start preparing? Right now! Because anything can happen at any moment. Just like we play, enjoy life and also take time out for studies everyday, regularly remembering we have an exam coming up at some point, similarly, while doing other activities, we must also take time out to prepare for our life's final exam. Good things should never be procrastinated. We do not prepare for an exam just the day before. It leads to unwarranted stress and regret. In the end, we only regret the chances we did not take.

The classic example of life's uncertainty is that of King Parikshit's, who was the grandson of the Pandavas. The Shrimad Bhagavatam's first canto explains: He was powerful, young, wealthy, youthful, famous, the ruler of the world, belonged to an illustrious lineage, and had everything that anyone could ever aspire for. And suddenly, one day, he got a curse that he would die within seven days from the bite of a snake–bird named Takshak. Does that sound familiar?

Everything is going so well and suddenly we face a huge reversal that turns our world upside down. What is our instant reaction? Stress, restlessness, anxiety, fear and the blame game!

However, the way King Parikshit responded is exemplary. He did not react. He simply accepted it as the mercy of the Lord. He was already well-trained in spiritual values by his illustrious grandfathers and, thus, it was not very difficult for him to make sense of what had just happened in his life. He firmly fixated on the truth. What he did after hearing the news of his imminent death is extraordinary and something we all must learn from. He taught us the best art of responding to an unexpected calamity and the perfect art of dying.

He knew what was to be done at this crucial moment. He immediately handed over the throne to his son Janmejaya and left everything to sit on the banks of the Ganges to immerse himself fully in the remembrance of the supreme Lord Krishna by hearing and chanting His glories and pastimes. The news of his retirement to the Ganges spread all over the universe. The great devas, sages like Narada and Vyasa, the munis, and saintly kings, all assembled knowing that something wonderful was going to happen as a great devotee of the Lord was about to leave his body. Eventually, the famous son of Vyasa, Shukadeva Gosvami, appeared to speak to King Parikshit, who had a great desire to spend the rest of his limited lifetime simply hearing about Lord Krishna. Right at the outset, King Parikshit asked a question that is so very relevant to all of us. As noted in the Shrimad Bhagavatam [1.19.37], he asked

atah pricchami samsiddhim
yoginam paramam gurum
purushasyeha yat karyam
mriyamanasya sarvatha

(You are the spiritual master of great saints and devotees. I am, therefore, begging you to show the way of perfection for all persons, and especially for one who is about to die.)

Shrimad Bhagavatam [1.19.38] explains,

yac chrotavyam atho japyam
yat kartavyam nribhih prabho
smartavyam bhajaniyam va
bruhi yad va viparyayam

(Please let me know what a man should hear, chant, remember and worship, and also what he should not do. Please explain all this to me.)

Shukadeva Gosvami congratulated Parikshit on asking such a glorious question, as the answer to it is the prime subject matter of hearing for all persons and it is approved by great souls. As Shrimad Bhagavatam [2.1.5] explains

tasmad bharata sarvatma
bhagavan ishvaro harih
shrotavyah kirtitavyash cha
smartavyash cecchatabhayam

(O descendant of King Bharata, one who desires to be free from all miseries must hear about, glorify and also remember the

Personality of Godhead, who is the supersoul, the controller and the saviour from all miseries.)

The Shrimad Bhagavatam [2.1.6] says

etavan sankhya-yogabhyam
sva-dharma-parinishthaya
aray-labhah parah pumsam
ante arayana-smritih

(The highest perfection of human life, achieved either by complete knowledge of matter and spirit, by the practice of mystic powers, or by perfect discharge of occupational duty, is to remember the Personality of the Godhead at the end of life.)

King Parikshit thus immersed himself in the topics of the Lord for the next seven days and nights and left this world in a fearless state, leaving a legacy for those who truly value their human life and wish to take it to perfection by passing the final exam.

However, the difference is that he knew he had seven days and thus could prepare well. We do not know how much time we have. Thus we should try and absorb ourselves in the hearing and chanting of the glories of the Supreme Lord regularly. This alone can help us remember Him all the time.

How was King Parikshit able to maintain a stable consciousness even when he heard the tragic news of his imminent death? Because he had practiced and prepared well throughout his life. Thus when the unfortunate news did come to him, he was able to see God's hand in this. It was because of his supreme dedication to spiritual culture. He spent his life serving the Lord while simultaneously carefully discharging his duties as a king and the news of his death was simply like the announcement of the final exam. Thus, he started preparing more seriously (as we all do when the final exams come closer) and passed with flying colours. He left this world remembering Krishna and attained the spiritual world, the divine abode of Krishna.

Life is not just about material advancement, but spiritual advancement as well. One day, everything we have worked hard for will disappear. The only thing that will matter then would be the spiritual credits we have accumulated and only that goes with the soul. Meditating on how everything will instantly end one day can open the doors to deep introspection as to how we are carelessly running around to gratify our senses. This opportunity is available even to animals. If our life also has to remain centred around eating, drinking and being merry, then how are we any different from animals?

Let us utilize whatever time and energy we have to prepare for the final exam and a better future life. Human life is precious. It is meant to rise above the four basic animal propensities of eating, sleeping, mating and defending. It is meant for a higher purpose. It is meant to prepare for our future destination.

Once a businessman was traveling to a distant place carrying a stock of goods on a ship. Unfortunately, the ship was hit by a storm and sank. The businessman barely managed to escape and swam till he happened to come upon an island. As soon as he reached the island, a huge crowd came running towards him shouting at the top of their voices. Initially, seeing them coming, he got scared but when he heard them shouting 'Long Live the King! Long live the King!' he asked, 'King? I barely managed to save my life.'

'Yes,' they said. 'You are our King.' They picked him up, put him in a palanquin, and brought him to their kingdom in a royal procession. He was enthroned as the king and started enjoying life to the fullest. 'Here I am,' he thought. 'I was about to die and now, all at once, I am the King.'

One fine day, his chief minister came and said something that shook him out of his complacency. The minister revealed, 'Dear King! You can only be the king on this island for five years. After this duration is over, those same people who carried you to the throne will forcibly pick you up and throw you in a dangerous forest infested with ferocious animals and demons where you will die a miserable death.' The king was scared for a little while, but being intelligent, gestured his minister to come closer and whispered something into his ear. Hearing what the king said, the minister immediately refused. 'Impossible,' he said, in utter shock. But the king told him, 'You better get going and do the work assigned to you. Else I am still the king and I will send you to that forest.' The minister bowed and left.

After five years, as predicted by the minister, everyone came, forcibly picked up the king, and started for the forest of uncertainty. But a surprise awaited them. They reached the spot of the unusual forest only to find there was none. Instead in the same place, there were beautiful palaces, gardens, ponds with lotuses, royal guards, and various communities happily settled there. Everyone looked at the King who just smiled and invited them over to live with him in the beautiful land. Everyone joyfully accepted the proposal and lived there happily ever after.

The businessman in the story represents us. The island is our body and the crowd that welcomed and carried the king represents our friends, family and relatives. The minister represents our senses and the forest transformed into a beautiful kingdom represents the spiritual world.

So what exactly happened? As soon as the king realized that he had a limited duration of five years to live on the island, he engaged his minister in preparing for his future destination so that when the destined moment did come, he did not have to worry. He could await a much more beautiful and prosperous kingdom where he was going to live a life of bliss forever.

Thus, just like the king, we also have a limited duration to be the owner of our body. We must remember this and utilize our senses with whatever time and facilities we have in preparing for our future destination.

And how can we do that?

We have five senses and they can engage in the following ways:

Ears or sense of hearing

In regularly hearing about the divine names, form, qualities and pastimes of the Supreme Lord from scriptures such as Shrimad Bhagavatam, Bhagavad Gita and Ramayana from the devotees of the Lord.

Nose or sense of smell

In smelling the Tulasi, flowers, scent or incense offered to the Lord.

Skin or sense of touch

By serving the deity, associating with devotees, travelling to holy places such as Vrindavan, Ayodhya, Mathura, Badrinath, and Jagannath Puri.

Eyes or sense of seeing

By regularly having a darshan of the beautiful form of the Lord (through a deity or a picture/painting).

Tongue or sense of taste

By chanting the holy names (such as the Hare Krishna mahamantra) and tasting the food that has first been offered to Lord Mukunda (Krishna, the giver of mukti or liberation).

Throughout the chapter, we discussed life being a preparation and if we engage in the above-mentioned activities daily, it is more than enough of a preparation for the final exam of death. These activities will help us attain divine consciousness. If we are engaged in them all through our life, we will acquire divine consciousness and attain the eternal kingdom of God after we leave this world. The Shrimad Bhagavatam [2.3.17] says

ayur harati vai pumsam
udyann astam cha yann asau
tasyarte yat-kshano nita
uttama-shloka-vartaya

(Both by rising and by setting, the sun decreases the duration of life of everyone, except one who utilizes the time by discussing topics of the all-good Personality of Godhead.)

Thus for a person dedicated to the service of Krishna, death is not the end but the beginning of eternal, blissful life. It is not an obstacle, but rather a stepping stone to the spiritual world where every word is a song and every step is a dance. The land of sweetness where the supreme Lord Krishna is busy playing His celebrated flute, tending countless wish fulfilling cows in the company of His cowherd friends, and the beloved gopis. As Sri Brahma-samhita [5.29] states;

chintamani-prakara-sadmashu kalpa-vrikshsa-
lakshavrteshu surabhir abhipalayantam
akshmi-sahasra-shata-sambhrama-sevyamanam
govindam adi-purusham tam aham bhajami

(I worship Govinda, the primeval Lord, the first progenitor who is tending the cows, yielding all desire, in abodes built with spiritual gems, surrounded by millions of purpose trees, always served with great reverence and affection by hundreds of thousands of lakshmis or gopis.)

IN A NUTSHELL

Attached to this body is materialistic, envisaging the end, going ballistic.

It's the fear that snaps us out of the rasp of reality.

It's the mental block that's bound to show us the mirror of mortality.

Dreading how this journey will end, will I have to be terrified at every bend?

An unfathomable fact to take in our stride.

Inside the material body, the immortal soul hides.

A spirited flame that will never extinguish, only this material body you will have to relinquish.

Life a blessed opportunity given to this eternal soul to grow.

Hold Krishna's hand and don't let this opportunity blow.

ACKNOWLEDGEMENTS

Nothing is possible without Lord Krishna's divine grace.

My first debt is to His Divine Grace A.C. Bhaktivedanta Swami Srila Prabhupada, founder-acharya of the International Society for Krishna Consciousness (ISKCON), who out of his causeless mercy gave to the world the permanent solution to all problems—Krishna consciousness.

I humbly offer my gratitude to His Holiness Radhanath Swami Maharaj, my spiritual master, for carefully nurturing the devotional creeper in my heart all these years with his selfless compassion, causeless mercy and personal example. His teachings, utmost care and concern for others' well-being are what I believe inspired this book and made it possible.

With folded hands, I profusely thank Radha Gopinath prabhu, Shyamanand prabhu, Gaurang prabhu and Gaur Gopal prabhu who always provided timely guidance during the turbulent times in my life.

I am extremely grateful to Prem Kishor prabhu, who, although a senior, has always acted more like a friend and heard me out patiently whenever I have had something to confide in.

Many thanks to Baldev prabhu, Vraj Chandra prabhu, Nanda Dulal prabhu, Radhadyuti prabhu, Radheshlal prabhu, Mukundmala prabhu, Brajraj Priya prabhu and Rasikacharya prabhu for always being there and making me feel comfortable and at home in the monastery.

I fall short of words as I begin to thank Resham Mehta and Sneha Makhija for helping me put the material of this book together. They have been of great support and extremely enthusiastic and meticulous in their work.

Thanks to Rashmi Jalan and Vandita Chawla for carefully preserving the content of this book and making it available whenever I needed it.

Writing a book is one part. But the other and the most important part is getting it through to a publisher. I am extremely grateful to Kanishka Gupta (Writer's Side literary agency) for connecting me to HarperCollins India, my publisher. Kanishka was very kind in pursuing this project and making sure I get the best. Many thanks to him for being so passionate about his work.

I am forever indebted to Sachin Sharma (executive editor at HarperCollins India) for patiently guiding me through the entire process of publishing and helping me with an extremely dedicated editor, Shreya Lall, for the project. Sachin has been extremely tolerant despite the fact that I got really delayed in submitting the book. He came across as a very genuine and humble person and I thank him for that from the bottom of my heart.

And special thanks are due to our dear Radhika Anand, an extremely talented, deeply spiritual and genuinely humble teenage girl. I was so excited to see her writings and that led me to request her to write something for this book. The readers will experience the depth of her realizations at the end of each chapter, entitled as 'in a nutshell,' as she summarizes each chapter into a beautiful deep poem. May she be blessed with more and more spiritual advancement.

And lastly, I humbly bow down at the feet of everyone, including the readers, and seek blessings so that this book can make a difference to peoples' lives, put a smile on their faces and bless them with a divine connect to supreme Lord Krishna.

Thank you.

INDEX

ABOUT THE AUTHOR

Nityanand Charan Das, a spiritual counsellor and a practising monk at ISKCON Chowpatty, Mumbai, for the last sixteen years, is a disciple of world-renowned spiritual leader His Holiness Radhanath Swami.

Coming from an army background, his childhood dream was to become an army officer. But Krishna had other plans for him and orchestrated his life beautifully. Life led him to fail the NDA interview, despite being one of the best in the group, to become a mechanical engineer instead, and eventually, become a monk at the age of twenty-four.

Swami Nityanand wishes to assist the current urban scenario by aiding people in leading a life of purpose, fulfilment and satisfaction in their professional as well as personal lives. His message is simple: spiritual life is not a life of rejection, but one of connection. We do not have to give up anything, simply add this valuable dimension to our lives.

He educates a wide range of audience of all age groups, especially today's youth, including children and teenagers, to reconnect with their roots and lead simple yet happy lives. He travels extensively, giving insightful sessions on the ancient wisdom of the Bhagavad Gita, Shrimad Bhagavatam, Ramayan and Mahabharat in a simple yet profound way.

In addition to giving discourses in every major city of India and in countries across the globe, he serves in various capacities in deity worship, organizing festivals/events and pilgrimages, and as a kirtan leader through his outreach.

He has authored four books: *Bound by Love* (2021), *Icons of Grace* (2022), *Ask the Monk* (2022) and *Epic Tales of Wisdom* (2023).

HarperCollins Publishers India

At HarperCollins, we believe in telling the best stories and finding the widest possible readership for our books in every format possible. We started publishing 30 years ago; a great deal has changed since then, but what has remained constant is the passion with which our authors write their books, the love with [illegible]

[illegible]

[illegible]

Read.